Saving Our Lakes & Streams

101 Practical Things You Can Do Today

James A. Brakken

Saving Our Lakes & Streams
101 Practical Things You Can Do Today

ISBN: 13: 978-1519716910

ISBN-10: 1519716915

James A. Brakken
Badger Valley Publishing
45255 East Cable Lake Road
Cable, Wisconsin 54821
715-798-3163
TreasureofNamakagon@Gmail.com

Published by
Badger Valley Publishing
James A. Brakken
45255 East Cable Lake Road
Cable, Wisconsin 54821
715-798-3163

Badger Valley Publishing

An independent publisher for independent authors.

TreasureofNamakagon@Gmail.com   BadgerValley.com

This book is dedicated to all who have struggled to protect and preserve our surface waters and to all those future volunteers who recognize the value of providing clean, safe, healthy lakes and streams for everyone—today, tomorrow, and forever.

ACKNOWLEDGMENTS

This collection would be less than it is if not for the time and talents of those in my writing group, the Yarnspinners, a chapter of the Wisconsin Writers Association. And, for their good suggestions and proofreading skills, I thank my friends, Abett, Lorna, Emily, Lisa and Howie. Above all, I thank my wife, Sybil, for unfaltering confidence in my work and for helping in so many ways.

Finally, I owe much of what I've learned about leadership and conservation of our waters to fellow Wisconsin Lakes directors and colleagues in the Wisconsin Lakes Partnership. I hope this book helps deliver their message as well as mine.

TABLE OF CONTENTS

Unless otherwise noted, all writing and photography is by the author.

Acronyms used in this book include

BCLF	**Bayfield County Lakes Forum**
CLA	**Cable Lakes Association**
CBCW	**Clean Boats, Clean Waters**
DCALS	**Douglas County Association of Lakes & Streams**
DNR	**Department of Natural Resources**
LWCD	**Land & Water Conservation Department.**
NRB	**Natural Resources Board**
NWWC	**Northwest Wisconsin Waters Consortium**
SCLF	**Sawyer County Lakes Forum**
UWEX	**University of Wisconsin Extension**
USFS	**United States Forest Service**
VCLRA	**Vilas County Lakes & Rivers Association**
WCC	**Wisconsin Conservation Congress**
WCLRA	**Washburn County Lakes & Rivers Association**
WL	**Wisconsin Lakes, formerly known as WAL**
WAL	**The Wisconsin Association of Lakes**

FOREWORD

We all love our lakes and streams. Many of us want to live by them, fish in them, and tool around on them in our boats.

We mow our lakefront lawns to the water's edge, then wonder where the frogs and shorebirds have gone. Our outboard engines emit gas and oil into our waters, invasive weeds clog shallow bays, and algae blooms foul our beaches, degrading the purity of the very water that draws us here. Our neighbors' growling lawn mowers and barking dogs reduce the quality of our time spent here. Are you depressed yet?

James Brakken lives in Bayfield County, and has witnessed these insults and more. Far from letting this depress him, he has taken action, serving as director on local and regional lake association boards and as president of Wisconsin Lakes, an organization that mobilizes volunteers to advocate for lakes.

And he wrote this handbook, a book which—as its subtitle proclaims—offers *101 Practical Things You Can Do Today*. The key words here are *"practical"* and *"today."*

If you fish, hunt, motor, paddle, or swim in our waterways, you need this book. Whether you live in a multi-million-dollar home on Lake Geneva, have a seasonal lakeshore cottage, or simply spend an occasional weekend at a rental cabin on a lake up north, you need this book. *Saving Our Lakes & Streams* should be required reading for all state, county, and town officials, for those who plan a career in natural resources, and for everyone who treasures water recreation.

Whether or not you and I do anything to help them, our lakes and streams will always be here. Without our efforts, however, our children and grandchildren will inherit waterways with problems far greater than those we face today. Their lives and leisure time will suffer tomorrow because of our negligence today.

So, what are we waiting for? Grab this handbook, talk to your fellow lake lovers and let's get to work!

Dan Small
Outdoor Wisconsin & Outdoors Radio

Saving Our Lakes & Streams

101 Practical Things You Can Do Today

James A. Brakken

Whether we call them lakes, ponds, or potholes, rivers, brooks, cricks, or creeks, we love our lakes and streams. Cool, blue water reflecting sun and shore. Fish jumping, kids swimming, Man's best friend fetching Frisbees and sticks ... what could be better? Our surface waters offer year-round pleasure to wildlife watchers, anglers, hunters, boaters, swimmers, and those who delight in the unique aesthetics of water. Yes, we love our lakes and streams. Maybe, though, we love them too much. Perhaps we are loving our lakes and streams to death.

Is it possible that our desire to spend time by the shore or on our waters is putting them in jeopardy? Subjecting them to overuse? Unintentional abuse? Could we be so focused on absorbing their beauty, so determined to be in touch with Mother Nature, that we overlook inadvertent damage we may be doing?

During my two decades of service to local, county, and statewide lake organizations, not once did I encounter someone who would intentionally do harm to a lake or stream. Yet, we all do harm. Few of these injuries are brazen, such as allowing agricultural waste to be washed into our streams or dumping sand into a lake to make a beach—both unlawful, by the way.

Quite the opposite, the wounds we usually inflict are slight—often so slight that we fail to recognize them. They can be as minor as using the wrong dishwasher detergent or saving the lives of your leftover minnows by releasing them into the water. Though hard for many to imagine, the humdrum acts of pinching a lead sinker on a line or raking autumn leaves into the lake can cause harm. If the impact seems negligible, why be concerned? Because it's not the single act that threatens our waters. Rather, it is the cumulative effect of countless adverse actions that can spell disaster, even though most of these actions may seem inconsequential.

Some compare this to the famed fable of the straw that broke the camel's back. Others liken it to the ancient torture method, death by a thousand cuts. Even when far from the water, every time we wash the car in the back yard, toss a recyclable container into the garbage, or accidentally leave the basement lights on, we may be contributing, ever-so-slightly, to the harm being done to our surface waters.

However, just as the cumulative impact of countless numbers of slight wounds can do immense harm, the effect of as many efforts to protect our surface waters can only improve them. Thus, this book is less about the harm we do to our waters and more a source of simple ideas each reader can apply to help protect them. Along with these 101 practical things you can do to protect our lakes and streams, you'll find some background information to help understand the need. This collection of lake-saving suggestions is neither meant to scold or insult, nor is any reader expected to apply all the tips. Rather, consider it a list of practices intended to preserve and protect our surface waters.

So, what about the lead sinkers, leaves raked into the lake, and damaging dishwasher detergents? Should we stop? Could we stop? Yes ... and no. Yes, in that each of us should become more aware of the potential impact we have on our lakes, good and bad. And, no, we should not stop living our lives in order to preserve our waters. We should, however, become aware of the consequences of our actions, do what we can when we can, and, by example, encourage others to do the same.

Considering all our lakes and streams offer us, it seems a fair trade.

We are told those who forget the past are doomed to re-live it. A look into the history of our northern waters may help us understand issues affecting our lakes and streams today. And greater understanding will lead to a greater potential to protect and preserve our waters for future generations.

A Brief History of our Lakes and Streams

In Wisconsin, we owe our lakes, streams, and wetlands to the glaciers. Ten thousand and some-odd years ago, the most recent glacier covered northern Wisconsin and surrounding states with ice. Inching from north to south, this mile-high sheet slowly relocated earth and raked across bedrock before receding. As the climate warmed, the ice slowly melted, leaving thousands upon thousands of lakes in northern Wisconsin. Only Finland and a small region of Alaska have a greater concentration of natural inland lakes.

Across time, our lakes and streams slowly matured into healthy waters abundant with life. Meanwhile, the canopies of tall pines cast their lovely shadows over the north. Nomadic hunter-gatherers, whose ancestors had crossed the ancient Bering Sea land bridge from Asia, slowly migrated from west to east. For nearly ten thousand years they used our waters as travel routes, gathering fish, wild rice, and other goods along the way.

Although these aboriginal people had no lasting effect on lakes and streams, the next visitors did. European explorers found the Western Great Lakes states flush with wealth. Handsome stands of pine stretched across a landscape teeming with fur-bearing mammals. Below ground, minerals waited to be discovered. The French and English soon struck bargains with Native Americans, using the lakes and streams to transport pelts bound for European furriers. During most of the 18th and 19th centuries, the hides of beaver, otter, mink, and other fur bearers became America's greatest export, attracting more Europeans. Though this dramatically altered Native American life and culture, the impact on our lakes and streams remained negligible.

Enter the Industrial Age and Westward Expansion. Around the time a New York editor, Horace Greeley, wrote in an editorial, "Go west, young man," foresters and economists estimated that there was so much white pine in northern Wisconsin, it would take a thousand years to harvest it all. However, they neglected to consider the rapid development of Heartland cities and their need for lumber. They also overlooked developing technologies related to timber harvest and the drive of those intent on converting an overabundance of trees into great wealth. The pine—a thousand years' worth—was gone in fifty, leaving behind the first major, lasting impact to our waters since the last glacier receded ten thousand years earlier.

Perhaps the effects of the great timber harvest first appeared when men began altering northern rivers for the spring log drives. Obstructions such as rocks and fallen trees were removed using manpower, draft animals, even explosives. Streams were dredged, river courses changed, and dams built to raise enough water pressure for the log drives. After ice-out, when the pine was released and the dams opened, millions of thousand-pound logs thrashed and crashed downstream. They scoured out river beds and most of the life once there. Rivers once abundant with fish became near-lifeless waterways.

The second lasting impact of the great timber harvest resulted from the timber companies' leftovers. With the pine gone, brush sprang up between the remaining tops and limbs of the fallen trees. Dry conditions soon led to vast forest fires across the north. Many of these fires were deliberately set by land brokerage companies in order to clear land for farming. With no canopy, no understory, and a barren forest floor, rains quickly eroded the landscape, washing nutrients, sediments, and soot into our lakes and streams. Today, limnologists and other scientists who study lakes find a decades-thick layer of carbon and ash in the sediment core samples of most northern lakes.

What should have been a "thousand-year" timber harvest lasted only decades, beginning around 1875 and ending around 1925. And, although some forest restoration was done by the Civilian Conservation Corps in the 1930s and some lake and stream restoration occurs today, our lands were forever changed.

The third lasting impact to our waters soon followed.

4

Lakes previously used to transport logs and utilized as dumping grounds for sawdust and other industrial waste became recreational attractions. Locomotives that once carried pine, now brought tourists. Cabins soon lined the shores and, with no restrictions in place, wastewater pipes extended into our lakes and streams. The resulting nutrient-rich discharge over-fed our waters. Algae blooms turned some lakes green. Many waters became unhealthy, even hazardous.

Regulation followed but late, as usual. Although new septic dry wells and drain fields kept sewage from flowing directly into the water, this became a temporary fix as the nutrients leaching from tank to soil eventually worked their way into the groundwater, then the surface water. It would take another fifty years to analyze the problem and fine tune septic systems. Meanwhile, more and more lake homes crowded the shores of more and more lakes.

In 1909, a young mechanic rowed his wooden boat to a store to buy ice cream for his sweetheart. Rowing against the wind on the return trip, the ice cream melted. This inspired Ole Evinrude to build an outboard motor in order to ease the task of rowing. He had no idea what would result. At sixty-five pounds and sixty-two dollars, his one-and-a-half horsepower "knuckle-buster" outboard engine became popular almost overnight. Interest in this new technology quickly drove improvements as well as sales. A mix of gas and oil now did the work of back and arm muscles, allowing boaters to go faster and farther. Unfortunately, up to fifty percent of a common two-stroke engine's fuel went unburned and was exhausted directly into the water—a problem that still occurs today. Four-stroke engine technology and improvements in two-stroke motors have made them cleaner, but the problem remains, especially in light of rapidly increasing recreational boat traffic.

More traffic also means less space per boat and what has now been termed as "user conflict" on our lakes and streams. Additionally, the stirring effect caused by propeller-driven watercraft tends to disturb nutrient-rich sediments, releasing them and altering the lake ecology, even creating algae blooms.

Yes, Ole Evinrude had good intentions. But how could he know this new technology, the gasoline-powered boat, would lead to the fourth change in our surface waters?

The fifth change arrived from faraway lands. Exotic European and Asian plants and animals sequestered by thousands of miles of oceans, found their way to the Americas and into our lakes and streams. Some exotics like the lovely purple loosestrife reached our shores because well-intentioned immigrants carried them along as a reminder of their homeland. Others, like Eurasian water milfoil, were brought here to aid in the development of fish farms. Still more, like the zebra mussel and Round Gobi, came in the ballast water of ocean-going ships. With no natural controls on our continent to slow their spread, the invasive plants and animals prospered as unaware boaters carted them from lake to lake and stream to stream.

Reaction to the spread of aquatic invasive species (AIS) came slowly. By the time scientists and conservationists realized their significance, many invasives had gained a strong foothold. Today's efforts to protect the last remaining waters from AIS often seem futile in light of the rapid increase of our population and the overwhelming interest in recreational boating.

The sixth lasting change to our lakes began during America's economic boom after World War II. The family car increased recreational time, while better wages gave many the opportunity to own a cottage at the lake. Large parcels were divided and divided again to accommodate cabins that soon dotted the shores—their owners imposing urban and suburban lifestyles onto rural landscapes. Forested waterfronts gave way to manicured lawns and impervious surfaces, accelerating the runoff of nutrients. The resulting increase in aquatic plant growth and decrease of water quality impaired most developed lakes and many streams. Today, small, previously undeveloped waterbodies are becoming rare, as those seeking homes on pristine, secluded waters target them for development.

Well-meaning anglers are responsible for the seventh lasting change in our waters. The quest to bring home the largest number of the largest fish tends to remove the best progenitors of the species. Over-harvest of the choice breeding stock presents an obvious risk to any form of life. The balance of fish species in many lakes has been upset by over-fishing the large, genetically superior breeders. This results in the absence of larger predatory fish and an overpopulation of stunted panfish. This change in the ecology of our lakes could be reversed. Today's relatively new practice of catch-and-release fishing is helping as gains acceptance among some anglers. Unfortunately, the desire to catch the most and keep the largest seems deeply ingrained in the behavior of many anglers.

These are the seven obvious, man-made changes our lakes and streams have experienced since Europeans arrived in North America. The eighth lasting change is occurring right now.

Since the beginning of the Industrial Age, our atmosphere has seen increases in carbon dioxide and other chemical compounds. Over time, some of these have entered our lakes and streams when rains washed them from the skies. Mercury and acid rain have altered many lakes and elicited health warnings regarding fish consumption in others. The greenhouse effect of a carbon-rich atmosphere has reduced the length of time ice remains on our northern lakes. Scientists now fear walleye, trout, and other fish requiring cold water environments will be supplanted by warm water species like bass. Many aquatic plants, including invasive species, are likely to change—and not for the better.

If these eight lake history lessons are learned and applied, we may have a greater chance of slowing many unwanted changes to our surface waters. If not, it is unlikely future generations will enjoy our lakes and streams as we do today.

The old Wisconsin Lakes motto holds true: *It's up to you to keep it blue.*

As the US population grew following WWII, prosperity and personal mobility increased. Many Americans invested in seasonal cabins. As the decades passed, families outgrew these small lakeside cottages. Large lake homes took their place, lining our shores. The seasonal cabins of the fifties became the half-million-dollar-or-more waterfront homes of today.

Next, clearing, mowing, and fertilizing of lawns added new nutrients to the soil. Paved drives, large rooftops, and other impervious surfaces resulted in increased runoff, carrying both nutrients and sediments to the lake. These altered the water chemistry, brought algae blooms, changed aquatic plant life, and affected fish and near-shore wildlife populations. Our lakes changed forever.

1
IT'S UP TO YOU TO KEEP IT BLUE

Give a Hoot

Litter destroys nature's beauty. We've known this since the 1950s when America's roadways were a common dumping place for refuse. Subsequent anti-littering laws and citizen clean-up programs, such as Adopt-A-Highway, reversed that trend.

Unfortunately, year after year, our lakes and streams continue to be strewn with cans, bottles, and other trash. Fishing line is too often tossed over the side of the boat. Not only does it last almost forever, it can wreck an outboard motor when tangled in the prop. Worse, line often becomes tangled around the legs, necks, and beaks of our birds. Each year, many loons, shorebirds, and other wildlife die horrible deaths due to improperly discarded fishing line. Litter, whatever the form, belongs only in the trash.

What you can do:

1. Never throw anything in the water other than your bait when fishing, yourself when swimming, and the occasional skipping stone.

2. Lead by example, encouraging others to not litter.

3. If you find cans, bottles, or other litter in the lake and can safely remove it (with your life jacket fastened), put it in the trash.

4. Whether boating or hiking, remind your friends and family of the camper's motto, *if you can carry it in, you can carry it out.*

Historians tell us that in the 1880s, Lake Geneva, the first Wisconsin lake developed for recreation, became a popular place to build a second home because it was a mere one-day journey by horse-drawn carriage from both Chicago and Milwaukee.

Today, nearly all of Wisconsin's lakes are within a one-day "horseless carriage" drive from those major metropolitan areas and many other cities in Wisconsin, Illinois, Iowa, and Minnesota.

No Dumping!

Never dump fish remains or leftover bait in any lake or stream. This may sound odd, but fish taken from the water, if not released at once, must be considered part of the angler's daily bag limit. Your bag limit becomes your personal possession.

> According to a UW survey, 85% of Wisconsinites use our waters on a regular basis. Boating, swimming, and fishing are popular uses, but the prevailing on-the-water recreational activity is the enjoyment of the aesthetic qualities offered by lakes.
>
> In another Wisconsin Lakes poll, overwhelming numbers of respondents said their favorite activity was simply "looking at the lake."

According to state law, a person's possessions cannot be discarded into the water. Fish remains are nutrients. Science tells us our lakes do not need excess nutrition. Common sense tells us nobody wants to see dead fish left in the water.

Live bait is a special issue. Because your minnows are certain to have come from elsewhere, they may have slightly different genetic qualities than the native minnows. Introducing them to your favorite waters could alter the ecological balance.

Worse, your minnows might carry a virus. If released alive into the lake or stream, changes, unseen at first, could slowly degrade the fishery, even kill off beneficial species.

What you can do:

5. Always dispose of your minnows in the trash or far away from people and pets.

6. After cleaning fish, place the remains in the trash for disposal *away* from the lake. (During warm weather, some anglers wrap and freeze the remains until the trash is picked up.)

Stop the Invasion

Aquatic invasive species (AIS) such as rusty crayfish, purple loosestrife, Eurasian water milfoil (EWM), zebra mussels, and many others are altering North America's lakes and streams. Most came from other continents, some in the ballast water of merchant ships, others carried here by individuals with good intentions. Today, invasive aquatics are being quickly spread. We who boat and fish are the cause. Almost all of the transfer of AIS can be traced to people traveling from waterbody to waterbody with plants and animals on board. Many lakes and streams have been forever changed.

To compound matters, over the past century, many of our waters have seen a rise in the level of nutrients—some due to phosphorus-rich runoff from lawns, others from failing septic systems. AIS thrive, usually choking out native plants when water quality offers a surplus of nutrition.

EWM, for example, can completely fill a lake with a tangle of plants in only a few years. This tangled mass can prevent boating and swimming and ruin the fishing. Masses of EWM in Minnesota's once-pristine Lake Minnetonka caused at least two drownings after the swimmers became tangled in long strands of milfoil. One was a University of Minnesota swim team athlete in training. The lake is lined with lake homes that contributed to the problem by keeping the water rich in phosphorus for decades.

Recreation in EWM-choked lakes comes to a halt. Property values plummet. We must do all we can to prevent the spread of AIS today if we want children to enjoy our water tomorrow.

What you can do:

7. Between landing and launching, clean and inspect your boat, motor, trailer, anchor, and fishing gear for aquatic plants and animals. Not only can they harm a lake or stream, transportation of plants or live aquatic animals on any Wisconsin roadway violates state law and can result in a hefty fine.

8. Encourage others to check their boating equipment. Remove all aquatic plants and animals.

9. Lead in the effort to stop the spread of non-native aquatic species by learning more about AIS through the Clean Boats, Clean Waters (CBCW) program. Their free workshops will train you to be a CBCW monitor. This training can help you recognize most AIS intruders so you can inspect your lake for invasive species. Be sure to report your volunteer hours to your local AIS prevention program coordinator. Your time can be used to build required matching funds for grants intended to prevent further spread of AIS.

10. Never use phosphorus-based lawn fertilizer and reduce runoff from non-impervious surfaces however possible.

11. Maintain your septic system. Nutrients from a poor system will seep through the soil and end up in the lake. Nutrient-rich water offers AIS a greater opportunity to thrive.

Septic Sensibilities

Follow these tips to keep your septic system healthy, save money, and comply with the law.

1. Avoid fines: Have your septic system serviced at least once every 3 years, per Wisconsin law.
2. Flush only human waste and toilet tissue. Anything else can result in system failure.
3. Protect septic lines and drain fields from freezing. Never plow or drive over them in winter.

Save thousands in repairs and keep your lake clean and safe by maintaining a healthy septic system. See your county UWEX agent for more information.

Compelled to Keep a Lake AIS-free: An Interview

Lake Namakagon lies in the southeast corner of Bayfield County. This 3,200-acre lake is very popular, especially with fishermen. Much of the lake is shallow. Its large beds of native aquatic plants make great cover for fish. Because of its shallow nature and its close proximity to the 13 lakes and 3 rivers in Sawyer County that are contaminated with Eurasian water milfoil, Namakagon is at high risk of invasion from this devastating plant. DNR statistics show that, although any boat can bring invasives to a lake, it is the irresponsible or unaware fisherman who is likely to transport invasive plants.

There is good reason for concern. Many weekend anglers who come to northern Wisconsin visit three lakes a day. In the case of Bayfield County's lakes, it is a short hop through the fire lanes from nearby Sawyer County's contaminated lakes to yet-unspoiled Lake Namakagon.

The Namakagon Lake Association (NLA) vice president is known for the work he has done to keep invasives out of the lake. He writes AIS grants, supports stronger AIS laws, recruits volunteers to monitor landings, and inspires others to join in the effort to protect the lake. Thanks to him, when the Internet Landing Installed Device Sensor (I-LIDS) video surveillance cameras became an option, the Namakagon Lake Association received a grant from WDNR to install an I-LIDS camera.

I spoke with the NLA vice president (**VP**) to learn more about the association's work to stop AIS and just what compels him to work as hard as he does to protect Lake Namakagon. The following is the gist of our conversation:

JB: You're well known for your effort to protect our lakes from invasives. What's behind your personal drive to keep Namakagon AIS-free?

VP: Having grown up on Lake Minnetonka, I have seen firsthand what Eurasian water milfoil can do to a lake. Boating is curtailed, swimming is impossible if not dangerous, and there are literally no viable alternatives short of poisoning the entire lake, which Minnesota's DNR will not allow, to get rid of this particular invasive. My parent's home on Wayzata Bay is located on 100 feet of west-facing frontage just ten minutes from downtown Minneapolis. Mom and I used to go for a swim down the shoreline whenever we could and I will always remember those precious times we had together. That all ended, however, when Eurasian water milfoil ruined the entire shoreline.

JB: Do you recall how the Eurasian water milfoil spread?

VP: I first noticed it in Gray's Bay which is adjacent to Wayzata Bay. Due to boating activity, it spread rapidly to the rest of the lake. Now they use harvesters to try to mitigate the damage, but that also has the effect of allowing the milfoil to spread. It can establish itself easily in up to 20 feet of water.

JB: How did the spread of EWM affect the sale of your mother's Lake Minnetonka home?

VP: When the estate sold my parents' home four years ago, our realtor told me that were it not for the milfoil, the home would have sold for somewhere between $500,000 and $1,000,000 more than it did. At the upper end of the scale, that represents 33% of the value of the property. Waterfront owners can estimate the negative impact Eurasian water milfoil could have on their lake property at 30% or more. Nobody wants recreational property where swimming, boating, fishing, and even jet skiing are inversely impacted!

JB: By my count, Lake Namakagon has over 400 waterfront homes in addition to all the resorts on the lake, not to mention all the undeveloped property. The total value must be near a half-billion dollars, making the property tax somewhere near $5 million annually. Cut by 30%, it would result in a loss of $1.5 million in property tax revenue. Imagine what that would do to the county and town services here in Wisconsin.

VP: That's why it is absolutely imperative that all of our town and county officials do everything they can to support the efforts to stop invasives *before* they arrive at our lakes.

JB: The NLA's latest DNR Lake Planning Grant will purchase two new I-LIDS cameras. It specifies that the lake association must provide trained Clean Boats, Clean Waters inspectors at the launch sites. How will the NLA handle this?

18

VP: We will have a mix of paid and volunteer inspectors. We already have a few trained monitors. Finding more volunteers is up to the current NLA Board but, from past experience, it's like pulling teeth. Hence, the dependence on the I-LIDS systems.

JB: Some folks simply don't have the time and won't give up a day at the lake to spend at the landing. What would you say to them?

VP: I'd tell them that after invasives are established, when they finally get "religion" and it's too late, well, good luck selling their property or enjoying their lake. If they can't give up one day each summer for the good of the lake, they should donate enough to cover the wage of a paid monitor for one day. In fact, every person on every lake should do this. If your lake association hires monitors to inspect for invasives, you should either give one day's worth of time or donate a CBCW monitor's wage for a day. It's a small price to pay for protection of your property value and the future of your recreation.

JB: Why not just let EWM come, then get the government to clean it up?

VP: Because even if the DNR had the money, which it doesn't, there is no way to effectively treat this stuff. Plus, once EWM is in the lake, it's there for good. It will always come back—always! The *only* defense is prevention.

JB: When was the first I-LIDS landing camera installed?

VP: Three years ago. We review the videos as does Environmental Security Systems, the manufacturer of the I-LIDS equipment. They provide various monitoring options.

JB: Do you think these cameras make a difference in the boater's behavior?

VP: I know they do for a fact. The videos prove it. It's not uncommon to see people get out of their vehicles, peer into the camera lens, look back at their boat, and then go inspect it. Of course, we've seen other interesting behavior that I'll not comment on. Some is pretty hilarious. Needless to say, they (the I-LIDS cameras) do have a positive impact. Are they intimidating? Perhaps. But so what? They're not as frightening as a lake choked with thick mats of milfoil!

JB: Some boaters say the I-LIDS cameras are just one more invasion of privacy by the government. How do you respond to this claim?

VP: Obey the law and you will have nothing to worry about. But know this: the Bayfield County District Attorney has personally advised me that citations can be issued based on photographic evidence. The law will be enforced.

JB: Wisconsin has tightened up the "no-transport" laws, making it illegal to have attached plants and animals on boating equipment when on any roadway. What effect do you think this will have on boaters?

VP: It's a great improvement and we have our local state senator, Bob Jauch, to thank for that as well as the Great Lakes Compact. Senator Jauch is a great advocate for the environment.

JB: The Bayfield County Lakes Forum succeeded in getting the first AIS transport law passed in Wisconsin, then later got the penalties increased and helped get the legislature to pass a statewide no transport law. What AIS issue would you like to see BCLF tackle next?

> "If (waterfront owners) can't give up one day each summer for the good of the lake, they should donate enough to cover the wage of a paid monitor for one day. In fact, every person on every lake should do this. If your lake association monitors for invasives, give one day's worth of time or donate a CBCW monitor's wage for a day. It's a small price to pay for protection of your property value and the future of your recreation."

VP: Fishing tournaments that allow their contestants to jump from lake to lake during their events. That should be either monitored at tournament expense for compliance with Wisconsin statutes or banned outright.

JB: Where do you think this is all headed? What's your vision of this lake in 20 or 50 years?

VP: It depends on the people who enjoy our lakes. If they educate themselves about AIS, clean their equipment, support the programs by volunteering or donating and teaching their kids to do the same, we can keep our lakes clean and healthy until we find effective treatments for invasives. But it takes everyone.

JB: What's your parting statement to the waterfront property owners who will read this interview?

VP: First, don't wait until EWM comes to your lake. Learn all you can about the problem now. Second, follow the AIS laws and make sure every boat you launch is AIS-free and make sure your friends and family do the same. Third, support your local AIS program by volunteering and donating a few bucks through your lake association. Don't rely on others. Please get involved lest you live to regret it! It's really up to you.

See EnvironmentalSentry.com for more images plus video clips of I-LIDS cameras in use. The website also has a tool that allows you to calculate the potential risk of AIS contamination faced by your lake. To see if your favorite lake has EWM, visit http://dnr.wi.gov/lakes/invasives/AISLists.aspx?species=EWM& groupBy=Species where you can search by county or by lake.

(More on I-LIDS on page 135.)

On the Other Hand ...
Who Should Pay for our AIS Protection Programs?

In northern Wisconsin we place high value on water recreation and clean, healthy lakes. Water quality is very important to our tourism-based economy. We also know that Eurasian water milfoil (EWM) and other aquatic invasive species (AIS) hitchhike from lake to lake on boating equipment and are now at our doorstep, threatening our waters.

Fishing boats trailered from boat launch to boat launch are the primary cause and greatest reason for concern. Local anglers are not the problem and not likely to spread invasives. Local folks know the rules and risks. They want to protect the waters near their homes and communities. In fact, local anglers and seasonal residents are our best allies when it comes to protecting area lakes from invasives. Often, it is the ill-informed or irresponsible transient boaters who are likely to spread AIS. They come for a weekend or a short vacation, visit several lakes, then depart, often leaving problems behind for others. They have no ownership in our northern lakes, no reason to care what troubles they may cause for others and our lakes. Their only concern is a full stringer and fun. According to a WDNR survey, the typical traveling angler out for a weekend fishing trip will visit an average of three lakes each day before returning home. Some of those lakes may contain AIS. They often don't know. Too often, they don't care.

Transient fishermen are the primary reason we must monitor our boat landings if we want to keep our lakes clean and healthy. This effort started over a decade ago with volunteers doing this work. But it soon became clear that, although these much-appreciated volunteers help, it takes *paid* landing monitors, working on a regular, dependable schedule, to educate boaters, check boating equipment, and slow the spread of AIS.

The State of Wisconsin knows this, too. That's why the DNR offers substantial matching grants to counties, towns, and lake organizations to help pay landing monitors' wages. But who should contribute the necessary matching funds to qualify for these grants? Here are four options:

- **Some feel it is the taxpayers' responsibility.** After all, isn't it *everyone's* duty to take every step possible to protect our natural resources? On the other hand, only a small percentage of the taxpayers actually spend much time on the water. And don't they already contribute taxes toward the state share? Should the taxpayers have to cover this bill, too?

- **Some say the waterfront owners should pay the match amount.** After all, they get to live on the lake. On the other hand, waterfront taxes are already very high and waterfront owners pay far more taxes than others. Besides, these folks are not the ones who are likely to spread invasives. Most are aware of the issue. Most use the landing only twice a year, once to launch in the spring and again to land in the fall. Should they really be asked to pay for a problem they don't cause?

- **Some think the business community should cover the match amount for the AIS grants.** After all, they profit from our clean, healthy lakes and water recreation opportunities. If our lakes are ruined by invasives, the tourists will go elsewhere, as will their money. Shouldn't the many business firms that profit from clean, healthy lakes bear the responsibility? On the other hand, our businesses are already asked for contributions to many community projects. And a few of our smaller local businesses simply can't afford it.

- **Some say the boaters who use the landings are responsible for the cost.** Many are accustomed to paying launch fees on other lakes. For example, Big Cedar Lake in southern Wisconsin charges $7 and Shell Lake asks $5 a day. In Bayfield County, both Twin Bear and Delta Lake campgrounds have a $5 launch fee to help match the AIS program grant. These are successful programs and seem to be well-accepted by boaters. Most boaters don't mind a small user fee for a day on the lake. After all, they pay when they golf, bowl, attend a Twins, Cubs, or Packers game, eat at a restaurant, take in a movie, and drink at a tavern. For less than the cost of a few dozen minnows or several gallons of gas, they get to enjoy a day on a clean, healthy lake. On the other hand, these folks help our

economy by spending their vacation dollars here. Should *they* be asked to pay to fish and boat, too?

So what is fair? Who should pay? Maybe there is no single answer. Maybe the best solution is to have all four groups pitch in. After all, *if everyone does a little, no one needs to do a lot.* A small charge at the landing, perhaps a couple of dollars, wouldn't hurt much. Discounted season permits would make it easy for local folks to afford. Small subsidies from our local governments and reasonable contributions from local businesses along with donations from the folks who live on the lakes would bring in all the funds needed. Keep in mind, AIS prevention is essential and every dollar earned is matched by the state, often three to one.

On the other hand, we can all sit back and hope someone else takes care of the problem. We can risk letting our lakes become unpleasant, green, weed-choked, almost-dead lagoons, like so many infested waterbodies in southern Wisconsin, Minnesota, and elsewhere. We can watch our northern tourism-based economy fail, stores, restaurants, and resorts close, then struggle to raise hundreds of thousands of dollars to begin the endless treating of AIS infestations, knowing our lakes will never be AIS-free again.

We can each pay a little now to keep invasives out or we can pay a whole lot later just to manage infested lakes. Our water recreation and local economy depend upon our decision. After all, Wisconsin's lakes belong to *all* of us. It's up to *all* of us to care for them.

AIS contributions can be made to your local or countywide lake association and may well be the best possible investment of your recreational dollar. Your county AIS coordinator can provide the contact information or visit the UWEX–Lakes Lakelist where you'll find lake associations in your region.

(http://www.uwsp.edu/cnr-ap/UWEXLakes/Pages/default.aspx)

Back when Wisconsin's fine for possessing an illegal deer was less than $200, poaching was significant. When the fine was increased to $2,000 and possible loss of license, gun, freezer, and even the vehicle used in the act, violations quickly became rare and have remained so.

Although shameful, poaching a deer is minor compared to what some boaters do when they transport aquatic invasives to our waters. The public pays the price—hundreds of thousands of dollars—to treat, but never restore an AIS-infested waterbody.

We need to do for our waters what we did for our deer if we hope to change the behavior of boaters who still transport invasive aquatic plants and animals to our lakes and streams.

Changing Behavior: The Need for an Increase in the Aquatic Invasive Species (AIS) Transport Penalty

On June 28, 2008, while training a volunteer, a northwest Wisconsin CBCW landing monitor discovered a boat carrying Eurasian Watermilfoil (EWM) as the owner prepared to launch. The invasive aquatic plant was lodged in his electric anchor. This fellow, who last boated in EWM-infested Lake Minnetonka, Minnesota, was given a stern warning and educated about the new county and state laws regarding transport of aquatic invasive species (AIS). Nonetheless, he returned in July, again carrying EWM from Lake Minnetonka. It was in plain sight, hanging on the side of his trailer. Anyone walking around the boat would have easily spotted it. It was clear that he had not taken the trouble to check his equipment in spite of being warned only weeks earlier. The Bayfield County Sheriff's Recreational Officer was called in. He informed the boater about the violation and fine. I was there. I spoke with him and saw that this news did not seem to faze him in the least. *He knew that the fine would be less than the cost of the tank of gas he used to come there to fish.* This "slap on the wrist" penalty seemed to have little effect.

Clearly, if we hope to protect Wisconsin Lakes from contamination by EWM and other invasives, we need *substantial* penalties that change the behavior of those who refuse to inspect and clean their boats. For this reason, I proposed that for a *second* conviction of illegal transport of aquatic plants and/or aquatic invasive species, the offending boater should face mandatory suspension of boat registration, fishing license, and waterfowl stamp in addition to a substantial fine. I believe such a penalty would all but eliminate the reason for any repeat offenders to trailer a boat. It would halt them from continuing their careless, irresponsible behavior. I have proposed this to state and county officials and continue to work to make this happen.

All who use our waters, both now and in the future, would benefit from this behavior-changing measure. It would be well-received by lake associations, communities, and conservationists concerned about the future health of our lakes. It would also be welcomed by almost all fishermen because sportsmen don't want their waters contaminated. It is very likely that the general public would support this "behavior changing" aquatic invasive species transport penalty, too.

Perhaps the only resistance will come from those few irresponsible boaters who are too careless or lazy to check their boats and don't care about the future of our waters. They won't like the new penalty because they know they are most likely to receive it.

My wife was the CBCW landing monitor who intercepted the EWM-carrying boater at the boat landing. Curious about the source of the invasive plant she found, we drove to EWM-choked Lake Minnetonka one August Sunday. At the Gray's Bay Landing, we were astonished to see the volume of traffic. The parking lots were packed. We saw long lines of vehi cles with boat trailers waiting to launch while many others landed their boats. Gray's Bay Landing is very wide, allowing multiple boats to launch and land at once. All lanes were filled all afternoon. Many of the boaters leaving the lake pulled the EWM plants from their boats and trailers. But some just ignored it. There were signs warning of EWM and other AIS in the lake but no landing inspectors or DNR staff on hand to assure adherence to the law. We learned a warden had been there for a while in the morning. It was the same story at a smaller Lake Minnetonka landing we visited, except we were told that it had been several weeks since a warden or any other landing monitor had been there. With thousands of boats leaving the Twin Cities lakes and other contaminated Minnesota and Wisconsin waters each summer day, the need for a *real* penalty for aquatic plant transport law violations is clear.

In July, 2009, the Wisconsin DNR Secretary, several legislators, lake association representatives, and other key players in the AIS prevention effort met in Hayward, Wisconsin for a roundtable discussion of aquatic invasive species control. There, they listened with interest to my proposal for stiff fines for repeat offenders of the transport laws. Delegates to the Wisconsin Conservation Congress who serve northwest Wisconsin unanimously approved my resolution calling for this change, too. Yet our government leaders have remained mute on this issue. It is imperative they tighten the penalties, if for no other reason, the cost to the public. Seventy-five thousand dollars was recently earmarked for AIS treatment of Sandbar and Tomahawk lakes in western Bayfield County (254 total acres). Another $200,000 was spent on the Minong Flowage, not far to the south. About two million dollars is needed to treat the EWM infested lakes in Sawyer County but the funds are not available.

> "We need to do for our waters what we did for our deer if we hope to change the behavior of boaters who transport aquatic invasives."

All these waterbodies got their EWM from careless boaters. Each infested waterbody poses a threat to neighboring surface waters as boaters come and go. Across our water-rich northern lake region, public funds are being pumped into our lakes and streams for EWM treatments.

And, notice I use the word "treatments." All of the money spent on Eurasian water milfoil infestations will need to

29

be spent again and again. This is because there is no sure cure—no way to completely eradicate it once it gains a foothold. The cost to the public is astounding.

Considering all that we now invest in AIS prevention and treatment of contaminated waters, and considering the value of our recreational waters and what's at stake when a careless boater contaminates another lake, it's time to put real teeth behind the aquatic plant transport laws. *It is time for mandatory suspension of boat registration, fishing license, and waterfowl stamp in addition to a mandatory, substantial fine for a second conviction of the transport laws. Third offense? Perhaps permanent revocation, confiscation of boating equipment, and jail time.*

Again, we need to do for our lakes what we did for our deer if we hope to change the behavior of those few remaining irresponsible boaters who contaminate our waters. And we need to do it now.

Since arriving in Lake Minnetonka, MN in 1987, EWM has spread throughout the lake, impairing boating and swimming in many areas, stopping it in others. Two drownings have occurred after the swimmers became entangled in Minnetonka's EWM. One was a University of Minnesota swim team athlete.

Waterfront owners have seen a reduction in property values up to 50% because of EWM.

During the boating season, hundreds, sometimes thousands of boats launch and land each day on Lake Minnetonka. Some of these boats carried EWM to many other lakes in Minnesota and to Wisconsin, a state that now has over 800 lakes afflicted with EWM.

2
SAVORING NATURE

Sound Advice

Many of us are attracted to our lakes and streams because of their distinctive beauty. We are intrigued by aquatic plants and animals above and below the surface. And the enchanting movement of nature reflected in shimmering waves fascinates us. But their beauty goes beyond what we see. We feel the cool water when we wade or swim. We smell the freshness of a lake breeze. In fact, all our senses enhance our experience, including our hearing. Nowhere more than by water are the marvelous sounds of nature revealed. In fact, the flat surface of a quiet lake or river allows sound to carry farther, thus increasing the experience of these sounds.

However, human activity can easily overpower the sounds of nature. For example, the roar of a chainsaw or sounds of other power tools early in the morning or late afternoon and evening may intrude upon others' enjoyment of the water. Blaring music and the incessant barking of a dog can be equally disturbing.

What you can do:

12. Make every effort to reduce noise whenever possible, especially in the late afternoon and early evening when many others on our lakes and streams enjoy the sounds of nature.

13. Always remember that sound carries farther over water.

14. The joyous sounds of kids playing on the beach might be music to your ears, but maybe not your neighbor's. We have two simple rules for kids swimming at our house. First, talking while swimming is fine, but anyone shouting or screaming has to take a ten-minute timeout. Second, the only time we shout "help" is when we really need help.

15. In the summer months, try to avoid use of chain saws, lawn mowers, or loud power tools early in the morning or late in the day.

16. Save your fireworks for the July 4th weekend and never use them over the water.

17. Do any target shooting far away from the lake, perhaps at the local gun club. (*Never* shoot at or toward the water. You'll have no idea how far that bullet will go or where it will end up.)

18. Avoid using your outboard before breakfast. Use your electric motor or your oars, instead.

19. Quiet your pets. Barking dogs and quiet lakes don't mix. Watchdogs should be taken inside if they persist in barking at boaters. Consider an electronic training collar for your barky dog.

20. Turn down the volume on your stereo or TV. The noise coming from inside your house may not sound very good from across the lake, even though it's your favorite entertainment.

Sound Carries Over Water

A few years ago, my neighbor and I had a conversation while cleaning fish. Joe was on his dock. I was near mine. The content of our conversation I do not recall, although it probably centered on the morning's catch. What I do remember is that, although Joe was on his dock and I on mine, on this clear, calm morning we were able to converse in normal tone and volume even though we were over 200 yards apart. It was almost as though we were talking over coffee across the kitchen table.

Lake Acoustics

Many who are unaccustomed to being near a lake may be unaware of the unique and wonderful acoustics of water. In another environment, sound can be absorbed by grass, rocks, walls, trees, cars, and everything else that it bumps. A lake is different. The water surface reflects sound. The smoother the lake, the better and farther sound travels. This effect is amplified by morning and evening air inversions, making sound carry farther and clearer yet.

This unique condition can cause problems. First, we all need to realize that every conversation that takes place on or near water can probably be heard over a long distance. Family discussions and conversations of a sensitive nature should be kept within our walls. Be sure guests and youngsters are aware of this. Next, we must realize that what some consider *normal* sound may be noise pollution to others. To twist a phrase, one person's "sound" treasure may be another person's trash!

We all need to work to combine the unique and wonderful characteristics of lake acoustics with common courtesy. Throw in a handful of understanding, too, because on rare occasions we will hear sounds from an early morning construction crew, reports from a duck hunter's gun, a chain saw, or the bark of a watchdog on the job.

Surveys show the number one reason people come to our lakes is for peace and quiet. If we remember that sound carries better across water than land and we make an effort to control our noise, our lakes will sound more like they did a century ago. That's good for all who cherish nature and our lakes.

Photo by Sybil Brakken

Give 'em Space!

Our desire to experience nature often draws us close to the wildlife we enjoy, especially near our lakes and streams. However, animals may abandon young if stressed when we come too close. This is especially true of loons and many other nesting birds.

What you can do:

21. Maintain ample space between you and wildlife. If you must get close, do so with field glasses or a telephoto lens.

22. Obey the law. Harassing loons and other wildlife is a punishable offense.

23. Lead by example. Encourage others to give space to wildlife.

Watch the Clock!

Anglers, kayakers, and canoeists often enjoy our waters in the early evening and early morning hours when waters tend to be calm and wildlife more active. Unfortunately, high-speed boaters often discourage less aggressive watercraft from using the lake. The noise from their motors can also disturb life on shore. The solution is common sense and boating courtesy.

What you can do:

24. Whenever possible, active water sports, such as powerboating, water skiing, and jet skiing should be practiced only during midday hours.

25. Know your local lake regulations and obey slow-no-wake laws.

26. Remember, power boats must, by law, give way to sailboats, rowboats, kayaks, canoes, and paddleboards.

27. Courteous boaters never allow use of their powerboat to drive others from the water.

3
NIGHT SKIES ARE FOR STARGAZING

Turn Down the Light

Some of us recall being near a lake years ago, on a night lit only by starlight and moonlight, the water reflecting the Milky Way. Today, our ability to see the stars is fading as dusk-to-dawn lights obscure our view of the heavens and the waterfront landscape at night. Will our children's children only see the stars in photographs and planetariums?

Our desire to extend daytime activities into night led to the illumination of our streets, driveways, and yards. Photos from space now show every city glowing through the night. But the glare from lights, whether distant or nearby, obscures one of nature's finest beauties, the vision of the lake at night.

What you can do:

28. Shield all lights that can be seen from the lake and turn them off when not in use.

29. Rather than dusk-to-dawn switches, use motion detectors to control security lights and walkway lights.

30. Never use lights as landscaping features in areas that can be seen from the water.

31. Be aware of "light trespass," the condition where the light from one property falls upon or interferes with another.

32. Provide adequate light but don't "over-light."

33. Choose lights that meet your needs without lighting the entire neighborhood.

34. Glare is both the most common lighting problem and one of the easiest to detect and fix. Eliminate glare by shielding light fixtures so the direct rays of light cannot reach our eye.

35. Encourage others to follow Wisconsin's Sensible Shoreland Lighting guide, available from your county's University of Wisconsin Extension office.

36. Obey the laws restricting the use of lights along the waterfront.

Preserving the Beauty of the Night

During the day our waters are used for recreation. Later, artificial lighting allows us to engage in nighttime activities that would be impossible or unsafe under normal conditions. Whether it's boating, fishing, or simply sitting on the porch to read, our enjoyment of the night is enhanced by the use of artificial light.

But the increase in nighttime lighting makes it hard to see the beauty of the night. Stars easily seen decades ago are still there, though much harder to find due to the excess light we cast toward the heavens. Light trespass, a condition that results when one person's light illuminates another person's property, contributes to the problem.

Sensible Shoreland Lighting

Sensible lighting can minimize the three most serious problems along our waterfront: light trespass, glare, and sky glow. When we see light from a fixture itself rather than what the fixture is meant to illuminate, we are observing glare. Sky glow results from concentrated streetlights and signs. This occurs near cities where much of the exterior lighting shines directly upward, causing the sky above to glow. The glow from city lights disrupts the viewing of the night sky for many miles. Our focus should be to illuminate only what we wish to see.

Sensible Shoreland Lighting, a publication available from your county UW Extension office, can help us understand the proper (and legal) way to provide adequate, safe lighting at waterfront properties. Some of the tips in the brochure are to

- Replace dusk to dawn yard lights with lights on motion detectors.
- Shield outdoor lights so they illuminate only your property.
- Aim all lights *away* from the water.
- Provide adequate light for the task, but never "over-light."
- Turn off all lights when not needed.

Request a copy of Sensible Shoreland Lighting from your UW-Extension office or online at learningstore.uwex.edu.

The Splendor of the Lake Night

It's hard to match the beauty of nature, especially while at one of Wisconsin's many small lakes. The unique qualities of water, such as reflection, wave action, and rhythm, when merged with luscious lakeside terrain, cannot be improved upon by man. From break of day, our lakes offer stunning, picturesque views. But after dark, when all is serene, the moon and stars often provide the perfect amount of ambient light to give us a special gift—the splendor of the lake night. Whether from porch, deck, dock, or boat, our eyes absorb the captivating, mysterious, often exquisite evening vistas.

But wait! What's that shining on the shore? It's neither the soft glow from a cabin window nor the flicker of a fisherman's campfire. It's a solar-powered decorative light! Although a recent addition to man's decorating arsenal, these clever, little lights are mushrooming in numbers and styles. They may be inexpensive at the store but solar-powered outdoor fixtures are costly to our nighttime views of natural lakeside landscapes.

Today, cheap, solar lights are marketed not as pathway lighting, but as after-dark yard ornaments. Although some waterfront homeowners feel these lights are attractive decorations near their shore, many others disagree. These lights shatter the soft beauty of the evening lake views. To neighbors across the lake and boaters, the problem doubles as each individual light, when reflected on the water, appears twice. When seen from the lake, this becomes "light litter"—intruding on, not improving on, the splendid evening views.

Not only does decorating a dock or lawn with lights spoil the beauty of the lake at night, it is outright *illegal*. Although there is no regulation regarding the use of decorative lights in the back yard or near the driveway, *waterfront homeowners cannot legally use lights as lawn decorations if they can be seen from the water*. It's the law. * Across Wisconsin, waterfront lighting ordinances specify that "lights shall not shine onto navigable waters" and "where lighting is used to illuminate (waterfront) walkways, only fully-shielded, cut-off style light fixtures shall be used." Every Wisconsin county has specific regulations regarding waterfront lighting. Violations should be reported to your county planning and zoning department.

Prior to installing any outdoor lighting, waterfront homeowners must carefully consider this law and how they may be altering others' enjoyment of the pristine evening scenery. Driveways and back yards may be appropriate for such lighting, but not so the waterfront. Always bear in mind, it's not just inconsiderate, it is illegal. Your neighbors and others who value natural lake views will appreciate your consideration as they soak in the splendor of the lake night. When it comes to beauty, Mother Nature needs no help.

State law: *"Lights shall not shine onto navigable waters."**

All outdoor lighting on shoreland lots within 300 feet of the ordinary high water mark shall meet the following requirements:

a. Lighting shall be controlled so as not to shine up into the sky or onto neighboring property navigable waters. This may be accomplished with fully shielded cut-off fixtures, directing lights downward or by other effective means.

b. Where lighting is for security purposes or to illuminate walkways, roadways, equipment yards or parking lots, only fully shielded cut-off style light fixtures shall be used.

c. All illuminated signs for commercial purposes visible from navigable waters shall be turned off between 11:00 p.m. and sunrise except that signs may be illuminated while the business facility is open to the public.

d. All forms of flashing or moving lights shall be prohibited.

*Recently, WI Act 55 nullified some of the above language. Subsequent legislation may soon reverse or modify Act 55.

Up in Smoke

The beauty of fireworks flashing, flaring, and reflecting from still water may fascinate us, but science shows it's not good for our waters. The heavy metals that create brilliant blues, reds, and greens, are toxic, as are the other chemicals in the propellants that eventually drift to the waters below.

Additionally, many lake and streambeds are strewn with shredded plastic and scorched paper following a fireworks display. Because most fireworks are used at night, this toxic litter is rarely retrieved, often sinking to the bottom where it can harm aquatic life. Divers tell us that many lake bottoms are littered with fireworks refuse. Other remains wash up on shore, where the toxics do similar damage.

Fireworks create air, light, and noise pollution disturbing our serene lake landscapes and those who enjoy them. Fireworks that *leave the ground* or *explode* are not only dangerous, they are *illegal* unless accompanied by the proper *municipal* permit. Those fireworks stores you see on your way to the lake might offer a permit, but it will not be legal. In Wisconsin, *legal* permits must be obtained from the local government, often the town or village chairman or their designee.

Fireworks are not toys and not for kids. Annually, thousands of children end up in emergency rooms because of fireworks. Even the simple sparkler, commonly handed to a small child, will reach temperatures exceeding 1,000 degrees. Each year, fireworks cause wild fires, house fires, and injure many pets. Fireworks users place their personal liability at risk, especially if the fireworks are illegal.

Many local communities now offer state-of-the-art fireworks displays managed by trained professionals. They are safer, offer better displays than the expensive, illegal, roadside stand variety of fireworks, and far better for both woodlands and waters.

Remember, though fireworks may be pretty for an instant, the beauty of our lakes is forever.

What you can do:

37. Place the health and beauty of our waters as well as courtesy to others ahead of individual desire to launch fireworks.

38. If you must use fireworks, select only the legal variety often found in grocery stores.

39. Think "safety first!" Keep a fire extinguisher nearby and remember, fireworks are not for children.

40. Advise those who opt to launch or explode fireworks to do so only near the July 4th holiday, only with a valid local government permit, and *never* over water or after 10 p.m.

41. If someone you know uses fireworks near water, remind them to clean up and dispose of the litter properly.

42. Suggest others using fireworks to apply common sense. Bear in mind their personal liability is at risk, especially if the fireworks they choose are illegal or lack the proper, local permit.

43. Call your county sheriff's department to report questionable fireworks use.

> **Some say using fireworks is patriotic. There is *nothing* patriotic, however, about U.S. consumers sending millions of dollars to China for fireworks, then using them to pollute our woods and waters while risking the safety of themselves and others. There are many far more patriotic ways to celebrate that do not jeopardize our environment, economy, and safety.**

Fireworks and the Law

The sale, possession, and use of fireworks in Wisconsin are strictly regulated by state statute. Local ordinances may further regulate fireworks. The state allows the use of "grocery store" type fireworks. But, if they explode or leave the ground, a permit is required.

Permits offered at fireworks stores are *not* valid in Wisconsin. Fireworks permits can be issued only by a mayor, town chairman, or their designee. The permit allows the possession and use of fireworks only in that jurisdiction. The permit must specify the type and quantity of fireworks allowed and the location where the fireworks are to be used. The permit must also list the exact date when the fireworks will be used and the date of purchase.

A person who possesses or uses fireworks without a permit is subject to a forfeiture of up to $1000 per violation. Each firework illegally possessed may be a separate violation. Parents or guardians who allow minors to possess or use fireworks may also be charged.

Fireworks litter must be promptly collected. Littering with fireworks is a separate offense with a substantial penalty. Lake litter from permitted, professional displays must also be promptly collected.

Call your county sheriff's department to report questionable fireworks use.

46

4
HOLD YOUR FIRE!

Never Shoot over Water

The warning on a box of .22 long rifle shells says "Range: 1 ½ Miles." Bullets from some high powered rifles are capable of traveling more than 3 miles. The risk of a bullet hitting an unintended target is compounded when the bullet strikes a flat surface, such as water. Like skipping a stone, shooting over water usually results in the bullet ricocheting, often several times. The shooter cannot tell where the bullet will go or how far, making this an extremely dangerous and irresponsible act.

An exception can be made for waterfowl hunters. Though caution is always required, the pellets in a shotgun have a range of less than 300 yards. They are also not likely to ricochet. Still, common sense and state hunting regulations must be observed. (Lead's impact on wildlife is addressed on page 61.)

What you can do:

44. Never shoot rifles, pistols, or shotgun slugs over water.

45. Always be sure of your target and what's beyond.

46. Encourage others to practice shooting only at approved shooting ranges.

47. Set a good example for youngsters by obeying all firearms safety precautions and state hunting regulations and by *never* shooting near water.

---

5 Rules of Firearms Safety

1. **Treat every firearm as if it's loaded.**
2. **Keep your finger outside the trigger guard until you are on target and ready to fire.**
3. **Always point the muzzle in a safe direction.**
4. **Be sure of your target and what is beyond.**
5. **Never shoot at or over water.**

Ashes = Algae

Ash, minerals, phosphorus, and nutrients left after burning leaves and garden litter near a lake or stream are usually washed into the water by rain. This runoff can directly increase algae growth, a common problem in many of our developed lakes. A bonfire on the ice has the same end result. But because all the residue from the bonfire ends up in the water, the impact is compounded. Ashes from your woodstove or fireplace are great for your garden but studies show that one pound of phosphorus can help produce 500 pounds of algae, possibly turning your lake pea soup-green. Ask your local warden and you'll learn it is illegal to dump ashes, leaves, and any other form of refuse into any surface water.

What you can do:

48. Rake leaves and garden waste to a location far away from the water where they can be naturally composted rather than burned.

49. Never dump your fireplace or woodstove ashes into a lake or stream and never burn on the ice where the nutrient-rich ashes are sure to end up in the water.

5

GIVE THE LAKE A BRAKE!

Throttle Back

Skimming across the water in a boat, personal watercraft, or on water skis can be exhilarating. No wonder hundreds of thousands of boaters visit Wisconsin's lakes and streams every year. High speed boating, though exciting, can be problematic for our waters when practiced near shore or in shallow waters. The effect of propellers churning up lake bottom sediments does more damage than meets the eye. Repeated washing of shorelines by wakes from boats results in erosion and often muddies the near-shore area. Marine and shoreland wildlife dependent on this area can suffer impacts we never see. Kayakers, canoeists, and others who enjoy recreation in less aggressive ways are often pushed from the water by dangerous wakes and waves.

What you can do:

50. Slow down for safety and protection of shorelines, shorebirds, native plants, and bottom sediments.

51. Limit your high speed boating and water skiing to deep water only, and then, far from shore.

52. Avoid "jackrabbit" starts in shallow waters and over weed beds.

53. Obey the 100-foot-from-shore slow-no-wake boating laws on all Wisconsin waters.

54. When power boating, use common courtesy when canoes, kayaks, and sailboats are present. Remember the 100-foot rule is a minimum requirement.

55. Urge your local government to establish no-wake zones on shallow, sensitive waters.

56. Request your local lake management organization to share this information with members.

Technological improvements in recreational equipment have changed the way we use our waters. Outboard motors that, statewide, averaged 4 horsepower in 1950, exceeded 80 hp in 1975 and 120 hp by the year 2010. Waterskiing, jet skiing, and other aggressive recreational activities, unimagined in the time of Ole Evinrude's "knuckle buster" outboard motor, are commonplace on many lakes today. Boat ownership continues to mount, although the number of boat landings remains the same, putting more and more boating pressure on our waters.

None of us would dream of polluting our favorite lake with phosphorus, right? Unfortunately, that is exactly what we're doing when we run our boats at full throttle in water less than ten feet deep.

Stirring Up Trouble

We live near a shallow channel between two lakes. It's common to see boaters zoom up to the channel, then, to protect their prop, throttle way down as they proceed toward the next lake. Minutes later, they zoom out of the channel. Slowly, the churned up water between our lakes begins to settle down once again ... until the next boat comes through. This is a common scene on our lake and many others across the north.

However, thanks to shallow lake education efforts in recent years, many boaters are now becoming aware of the damage that can be done not just to our props, but to our lakes. Most of us now understand the need for slow-no-wake zones. Because we care about our lakes, most boaters take it easy in the channels and shallow flats.

That's the good news. Here's the bad: The damage done by motorized boats goes well beyond the channels and shallows. Recent research shows that our props can easily disturb the water down to 10 feet. The wake behind our boat does far more damage than we see.

Researchers from the University of Central Florida conducted an interesting study on several small, shallow Florida lakes. Fishing boats with outboard motors crisscrossed the lake for two hours to simulate summer traffic. The disturbed sediments clouded the water slightly, not unlike many of our northern lakes on a summer afternoon. Readings were taken for both turbidity and phosphorus after the mixing was stopped. The turbid water began to clear immediately and was back to its original state in 26 hours. The phosphorus, however, cleared more slowly and, after 50 hours, had not returned to normal level. Nutrients normally settled into bottom sediments had been brought back into play by the stirring action of the outboard. And it took over twice as long for those nutrients to settle out

53

than it did for the water to clear. Research done on northern waters by the University of Wisconsin also bears this out.

We've all heard about the hazards of phosphorus. To protect our lakes, many of us make it a point to avoid high phosphate laundry detergents and other products. Most phosphorus-based soaps sold just a few years ago are now prohibited. Phosphorus lawn food is now restricted. None of us would dream of polluting our lake with phosphates, right? Unfortunately, that is *precisely* what we're doing when we run our boats at full throttle in water less than ten feet deep. Although we don't see the damage, it's there. We are feeding microscopic organisms that can store up to ten times their normal content of phosphorus. We are fostering the growth of algae, bacteria, and unwanted aquatic plants. We are altering the ecology of the lake.

This problem is greatly increased as the engine size increases. Although power boating, water skiing, and similar aggressive boating are the worst, all motors have the potential of increasing available phosphorus in the lake for 50 hours or more.

Row where you go!
Canoes, kayaks, rowboats, and sailboats are all lake-friendly. Grab your paddle. It's good for you and it's good for the lake.

The problem is also greatly increased when the number of boats is increased. It doesn't take long for several boats to thoroughly churn up a lake, providing excessive nutrition for unwanted plants and organisms.

How can we help? We can begin with our local lake management organizations. These citizen groups have the ability to educate members and visitors to the lake. Good lake management should include slow-no-wake rules in shallow waters. Lake organizations are in a position to encourage boaters to travel at slow-no-wake over weed beds, within 200 feet of shore, and in all shallow water. They can also distribute information encouraging aggressive boaters to limit jackrabbit starts and water skiing to deep water only.

Youngsters in our lake families should be guided toward non-aggressive water sports. Canoes, paddleboards, sailboats, and kayaks pose no problem to our lakes and streams. And they are safer for kids than powerboats and PWCs.

Next, we can encourage our town and county governments to place greater restrictions on aggressive boating behavior on our small lakes and sensitive water bodies. A 2010 law restricts boaters to slow-no-wake speeds within 100 feet of shore on *all* Wisconsin waters. The same limit applies to docks, rafts, and other boats. Town boards can create ordinances exceeding this.

To summarize, high speed boating and related aggressive water sports over weed beds and other shallow waters can cause significant, long-lasting increases in aquatic nutrients. The resulting algae, bacteria growth, and undesirable vegetation can have far-reaching effects, effects that could greatly diminish the quality of our lakes and streams. Individuals and our local lake management organizations can provide information, advocate responsible boating, encourage local government action, and contribute to the health and well-being of our waters. Boaters can help by avoiding shallow waters, observing the law, and using common courtesy. Throttle back! It's good for the lake.

Common Sense

Our lakes and streams offer a host of recreational opportunities for young and old. But with the many pleasures come some risks. Use common sense when on or near the water, especially when children are present.

What you can do:

57. Be sure all youngsters wear approved lifejackets whenever on, in, or near the lake.

58. When motoring, stay far away from swimmers, divers, and watercraft.

59. Make sure boats, trailers, and related equipment are safe and legal.

60. Don't drink and drive. Most boating accidents involve alcohol.

61. Fish and game laws and boating regulations are meant to benefit everyone. Follow them for safety, security, and protection of our lakes.

10 Most Common Boating Violations

1. Wrong number or size of personal flotation devices.
2. Operating boat with no valid certificate on board.
3. Operating boat in excess of speed limit.
4. Personal Watercraft violations.
5. Operating motorboat while under the influence.
6. Going too fast within 100 feet of dock, raft, or shore.
7. Operating boat at night without required lights.
8. No registration number or decal on boat.
9. Missing or unsecured battery cover.
10. Riding on gunwales or bow.

Save Your Vacation Dollars

Just when you're having a great day outdoors, it happens—you're cited for a mistake—an oversight—maybe a lapse in judgement. Here's what it will cost:

- Littering (includes cigarettes) — $200
- No boat registration — $200
- Improper boat numbers/decal — $169
- Illegal PFD (each violation) — $163
- Transporting live fish — $343
- Transport aquatic plants — $232
- Launching with aquatic plants — $295
- Failure to drain boat before leaving landing — $200
- Using live crayfish as bait — $243
- No fishing license — $182
- Out of season fishing — $263
- Over the fish limit — $243
- More than 3 lines or unattended line — $182
- 100-foot no-wake violation — $188
- Reckless boating — $200
- Underage boating — $163
- Tow skier without spotter — $173
- Boating at night without required lights — $175
- Missing or unsecured battery cover — $163
- Absolute sobriety (under 21) — $200
- Boat or ATV OWI — $453
- Snowmobile OWI — $658
- Fireworks violation — $200
- Burning without permit — $175

www.wicourts.gov/publications/fees/docs/dnrbondschedule.pdf

6
GET THE LEAD OUT!

The Problem with Lead

The debate is over. It is now widely accepted by the science community that lead is a toxic substance—perhaps, more toxic than mercury, a chemical we have greatly reduced in our  environment. Lead, because of its high toxicity, has been eliminated from gasoline and paint. Lead shot has been banned from use in waterfowl hunting. Lead sinkers and jigs are now illegal in our national parks and several states and countries. Still, lead's use continues to be allowed on Wisconsin waters.

Conservationists are concerned about toxins contributed to our environment, including the lead that ends up in our lakes and streams. Biologists are alarmed at the damage it does to our water birds, raptors, and so many other species.

Lead sinkers and jigs lost by anglers are often ingested by birds, resulting in a slow, agonizing death. Raptors and other wildlife feed on the resulting carcasses, suffering the same fate. Effective, reasonably priced alternatives are readily available.

The Wisconsin Department of Natural Resources has interest in reducing toxic lead contamination of our environment and has developed a plan to address the use of lead, but only in state agencies. And the plan does not affect the general public, including the anglers who use toxic lead sinkers and jigs.

Because scientific data verifies that lead poisons wildlife and because alternatives are available, the time is right for legislation to reduce the amount of lead used by anglers.

Non-toxic sinkers cost about a penny apiece more than toxic lead sinkers. For this small investment, every angler can have the peace of mind that comes with knowing that his or her sport is not killing off our herons, swans, loons, eagles, and other wildlife. If switching from lead to non-toxic sinkers and jigs will allow us to practice the sport of fishing without jeopardizing the health of our loons, swans, herons, and eagles, then how can we possibly say no? Simply put, this is just good conservation.

What you can do:

62. Stop purchasing toxic lead sinkers and jigs. Use only non-toxic terminal tackle.

63. Outfit youngsters' tackle boxes with non-lead items. They are nontoxic and far safer for kids to handle. Plus, inexperienced anglers tend to lose the most sinkers and jigs. Teach children to never put lead sinkers in their mouths or bite down on split shot. Use pliers, instead. Also, wash hands after handling lead. It is very important to remove lead residue from your hands especially prior to snacking on finger foods.

64. Place any small lead tackle you may have in a container, watching out for hooks. Deliver to any DNR office for proper disposal. Most communities also have toxic waste disposal opportunities where the lead can be recycled. Do not give your toxic tackle away to others or offer it in a yard sale.

65. Ask your local tackle shop to stock non-lead products. Suggest they showcase non-toxic sinkers and jigs instead of lead products, as is usually done.

66. Encourage your local lake association to sponsor free non-toxic tackle swaps so anglers can trade their lead sinkers and jigs for safe tackle.

67. Spread the word. Tell others about the problem and encourage them to switch to non-lead fishing tackle.

68. Distribute *Get the Lead Out* information cards to your friends, neighbors, schools and other community locations. Go to www.wisconsinbirds.org/getleadout.htm to view the card online and obtain cards for distribution.

69. Share this book with others.

One Lead Split Shot can
Kill a Twelve-pound Loon.

Lead poisoning is the primary cause of death for loons, herons, eagles, swans, and many other species. This happens when lost lead tackle is swallowed with small stones on the lake bottom to help birds digest food _or_ when lead tackle hooked in a fish is consumed by a bird. And lead-poisoned birds eaten by scavenging predators cause even more suffering and death.

Lead is one of the most toxic metals known. Many wildlife species suffer adverse effects due to lead exposure. _One lead sinker or jig can kill a 12-pound loon or 20 pound swan._

Going non-lead is a cheap and easy way for sportsmen to protect our waterfowl and raptors from lead poisoning. Alternatives to lead tackle are available in most bait and tackle shops. Anglers should request their tackle shops stock lead-free sinkers and jigs.

For complete article and info from LoonWatch, visit http://bayfieldcountylakes.org/?110970

> **Some anglers are unconcerned about this issue because they don't see the results of lead poisoning on our wildlife. Typically, animals that ingest lead will become very ill and find a place to hide from predators. The animal suffers severely and dies, never discovered by humans. There would be far less use of lead sinkers and jigs if anglers witnessed these scenarios in person.**

Over 30 years ago, paint manufacturers cried out when the EPA recommended removing lead from paint. Now, more paint is produced than ever before and it is of better quality. And when an American toy company recently imported some toys from China that were coated with lead paint, there was a loud public outcry.

The same will occur with lead sinkers and jigs one day. Of course, a number of anglers will object to the switch. But when word gets out that the alternative non-toxic fishing tackle works just as well and is reasonably priced, they will come around. Someday, it will be appalling to hear that an angler has been caught fishing with lead sinkers or jigs. Our  water birds, shorebirds, raptors, and other wildlife are eagerly waiting for that day to come. It may not be far away.

Will Switching to Non-toxic Tackle Help?
Nationally, lead poisoning of our waterfowl and secondary poisoning of the Bald Eagle resulted in a 1991 federal ban on the use of lead shot in waterfowl hunting. In 1997 alone, the U. S. Fish & Wildlife Service estimated that the ban on lead shot saved 1.4 million ducks. In Canada, a study showed a 50-70% decrease in lead levels in bones of waterfowl as a result of the ban in that country on lead shot for waterfowl hunting. These and other studies have demonstrated that switching to nontoxic materials does help protect bird populations and improve the environment.

The following appeared in the 2011 edition of <u>Lake Reflections</u>, the Bayfield County Lakes Forum newsletter. It is reprinted with permission from the author and the BCLF.

The DNR on Toxic Tackle:
Sean M. Strom, Wildlife Toxicologist,
WDNR Bureau of Wildlife Management

Lead is one of the most toxic metals known. Adverse impacts due to lead exposure have been documented in numerous wildlife species. Lead deposited in the environment will persist indefinitely and will not break down over time into less toxic compounds. Lead can poison people and animals including loons, bald eagles, trumpeter swans, and great blue herons. All it takes is one lead sinker to kill a twelve pound loon.

In 2006 the DNR implemented a Wildlife Health Program that included performing necropsies on every dead loon that was recovered in the state. Lead was identified as a major mortality factor for common loons and lead sinkers were routinely seen on x-ray images of lead-poisoned loons.

Lead poisoning from ingested tackle usually occurs in one of two ways: a lead jig head is swallowed by a fish which is then eaten by a water bird, or lost lead tackle is picked up along with small stones and grit from the bottom of lakes by water birds to help digest food.

Switching to non-lead tackle is a fairly inexpensive and easy way to make a difference. Alternatives to lead tackle are available on the Internet and in most bait and tackle shops. Consider asking your favorite bait/tackle shop to carry lead alternative fishing tackle.

LoonWatch (northland.edu/loonwatch) maintains a list of non-lead tackle suppliers. Other sources of information are the Raptor Education Group (raptoreducationgroup.org) and DNR's website (dnr.wi.gov/fish/pages/gettheleadout.html).

End of S. Strom article.

What is the Impact of the Lead we Lose in our Waters?

Lead poisoning has been documented in at least 25 species of water birds including herons, egrets, loons, ducks, and many more. Lead ingestion is a primary killer of both eagles and loons, symbols of Wisconsin's outdoors and cherished by nature lovers. Water birds pick up lead items along with the gravel they need for masticating food in their gizzard. Although mammals pass sinkers and usually live, birds digest them and die. One lead split shot is enough to kill a ten to twelve-pound adult loon and is 100% fatal if not treated. According to the Wisconsin Department of Natural Resources Wildlife Health Team, 26 Common Loons were submitted to their toxicity study team between 2006 and 2008. Approximately one-third of those loons died of lead poisoning from lead fishing tackle recovered from their GI tracts. (See photo.)

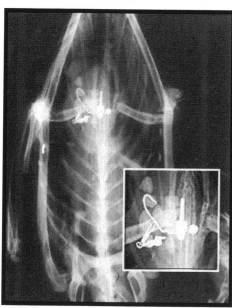

Research across the nation has found that poisoning from lead fishing tackle is responsible for more than half of adult loon deaths. In Wisconsin, lead poisoning is a significant mortality factor for the Trumpeter Swan. Of the 143 Trumpeter Swan carcasses submitted to the DNR for post-mortem examination between 1991 and 2007, 36 deaths (25%) were attributed to lead poisoning. Of 583 Bald Eagle carcasses submitted to WDNR between 2000 and 2007, 91 (16%) deaths were attributed to lead poisoning.

Minnesota DNR photo.

> "If switching from lead to non-toxic sinkers and jigs will allow us to continue our practice the sport of fishing without jeopardizing the health of our loons, swans, herons, and eagles, then how can we possibly say no? Simply put, this is good conservation."

Phasing Out Lead Sinkers and Jigs
Why a phase-out instead of an immediate ban?

Nobody likes being told that the law has just been changed and we must immediately comply. This phase-out will give bait shop owners and other merchants the opportunity to make adjustments and get used to the law. It will give anglers time to replace their small sinkers and jigs a few at a time instead of

requiring them to do this all at once. It will also give sportsmen a chance to adapt to the idea over time and for conservationists to educate folks about the need for the switch to non-toxic tackle.

Is all lead tackle included in the phase-out proposal?

No. Only small lead sinkers and jigs (under 1 inch and under 1/2 oz.) are targeted. Spinnerbaits and other tackle too large to be swallowed by birds are not included in this proposal.

When will this take effect?

The first steps of the process are already taking place. The DNR and several conservation groups are developing educational materials that will help anglers understand the problem and alternatives available that will both protect our wildlife and the rich traditions of sport fishing. Manufacturers are gearing up for what many feel will become a nation-wide trend toward lead-free tackle. As production goes up, the price will come down. Many anglers are aware of the danger associated with lead and have already made the switch. Lake associations in Wisconsin and other states are spreading the word, as are conservation and sports clubs. Public opinion is rapidly shifting toward non-toxic fishing tackle. The law requiring only environmentally safe sinkers and jigs won't be far behind.

How much lead do we put into our lakes?

The Minnesota Pollution Control Agency surveyed five Minnesota lakes for lead tackle loss. They concluded that over twenty years, sixteen tons of lead tackle had been accidentally deposited in these lakes, or about the weight of a semi-truck.

Are We Alone?

In a growing number of regions beyond Wisconsin, non-toxic tackle is already law. Bans on lead sinkers and jigs are now in effect in New Hampshire, Maine, New York, Vermont, and Massachusetts. Other states are exploring lead restrictions. USA and Canadian national parks and national wildlife areas have banned lead sinkers. Across the pond, Great Britain has banned lead sinkers. Denmark prohibits import or marketing of *any* product containing lead.

7
RESTORING OUR SHORELANDS

As the USA population grew following WWII, prosperity and personal mobility increased. Cabins, cottages, and summer homes soon lined our lakes and streams. Manicured lawns replaced trees, shrubs, and native flora. Many frogs, birds, and other wildlife no longer able to live near the shore disappeared. Fertilizers and sediments washed into the waters. The altered water chemistry resulted in algae blooms and allowed invasive species to flourish. Many waterbodies suffered varying degrees of degradation when well-intended people brought suburban style lawns to the rural lake landscape. Although recent zoning laws help regulate the clearing of waterfronts, earlier damage continues to harm our waters.

What you can do:

70. Just don't mow! Allow the natural landscape to return and flourish. Follow the laws restricting the cutting of trees, limbs, shrubs, and grasses in the near-shore area.

71. Restore your shore. If people wish to live on the water and in harmony with nature, our shorelands need to appear and function as close as possible to Nature's plan.

72. Maintain a deep and wide buffer zone along the waterfront. Think of it as your personal shoreland natural garden. When possible, try to exceed the required distance.

73. Build a rain garden to decrease flow of nutrient-rich runoff to the water's edge.

74. Ask your county conservationist or your local lake association to consider a Fish Sticks installation in your lake.

75. Consult your regional land conservancy regarding a conservation easement or a deed covenant to protect your property well into the future.

Shoreland Restoration: Six Reasons and Four Steps

Shoreland restoration means replacing a developed waterfront, such as a lawn, with native plants. Done correctly, this creates a buffer zone—a natural waterfront garden of native plants—to protect the surface water from polluted runoff. It also provides habitat for wildlife and beautifies the property when seen both from shore and from the lake. The many benefits of shoreland restoration include the potential to substantially increase property values. The greatest benefit is your enjoyment of a healthier lake.

Six Reasons Why

First, shoreland restoration protects our lakes and streams from nutrients carried in runoff. This reduces the chance of growth of aquatic plants such as Eurasian water milfoil, curly leaf pondweed, and algae. It can also increase water clarity. Whether you restore your own shoreline or persuade your local government to restore publicly owned waterfront, shoreland restoration is good for our surface waters. That's good for you and those who may one day become new caretakers of the lake.

Second, based on studies done in New Hampshire, Minnesota, and northern Wisconsin, shoreland restoration can increase property value as much as 7% for each foot of increase in water clarity. That could mean tens of thousands of dollars in value per parcel. This makes restoration projects very attractive from a financial standpoint.

Third, it's easy. In fact, it is easier to maintain a natural appearing waterfront than the traditional lawn that has been

> "When it comes to waterfront development, property owners who trade environmental quality for personal gain usually end up with neither. The trick is to use shoreland restoration to protect the environment while, at the same time, improving your property value."

71

"manicured" all the way down to the lake. This offers more time to enjoy the beauty of the property and less time with chores.

Fourth, waterfront owners can earn mitigation credits for restoration projects. Some county zoning departments will reward those who restore their waterfront by allowing near-shore alterations that otherwise would be illegal. Realizing the importance of restoration to the future health of our waters, some counties even offer property tax relief and other incentives for restored shorelines.

Fifth, *up to 70% of the funding for your shoreland restoration project may now be available from your county.* This is a great opportunity to improve your waterfront and protect your lake. There's no better time than now to begin your project. Contact your county's Land and Water Conservation Department (LWCD) for details.

Sixth, by restoring your waterfront you are setting a good example. Others will soon join in with their own restoration projects, thus beautifying the lake, improving water clarity, decreasing the chance of invasion by exotic aquatic species, and increasing everyone's property values. Everybody wins, including your family, your neighbors, the birds, fish, mammals, and your lake or stream. Think of this as part of your lake legacy.

Four Simple Steps

Step one is to put away that smelly, noisy mower! No more lawn chores. More time to play. More time to enjoy the lake and your yard.

> "Shoreland restoration can be very expensive, but it doesn't have to be. It's far better for both the lake and the property owner to follow a cost-free restoration process than it is to not restore at all."

Next, prepare. With or without help from a shoreland restoration consultant, you should create a plan. (See your county LWCD for a list of contacts and permit information.)

Begin with a rough sketch of your yard. Indicate where you would like paths, beds of ferns, wildflowers, decorative rocks, trees, shrubs, maybe even a rain garden or a bench for watching the sun rise or set. A list of plants and seeds native to the area will be helpful. Again, see your LWCD.

Consider cattails or semi-submerged logs along the shore to reduce erosion from waves and boat wakes. Although a few rocks strategically placed in the waterfront are acceptable, you should never rip-rap the shore. Rip-rap looks unnatural and can be a barrier to frogs, turtles, and other beneficial wildlife that need access to the shore. Plants you should consider include thorn apple or chokecherry trees to attract birds, pussy willows to attract kids, evergreens to provide some privacy, deciduous trees for shade, grasses and ground cover to cushion bare feet. Your plan should not include the removal of any native trees or shrubs already in place. They anchor the soil and take years to replace. A shoreland restoration consultant will have sources for native plants or can help you find them on or near your property. If needed, a consultant can also help create an instant, natural screen between you and your neighbor.

Step three: Prepare the planting site. Direct planting and good mulching usually give good results. Try not to disturb the soil or damage any existing native plants more than necessary. Sow your seeds, place your plants, then water, water, and water more. A half-inch of water each evening will have the plants thriving in a month or less.

Wire cylinders made from poultry fencing should be placed around deciduous trees or the local beaver family will soon drop in for an evening snack. Also, mark your paths so visitors don't trample your plantings. Again, water, water, water.

Important: Use no fertilizers, herbicides, or insecticides near the water. Be especially aware that no phosphorus fertilizers should come anywhere near the lake. It has a dramatic effect on unwanted aquatic plant and algae growth. This is why the sale and use of phosphorus-based lawn food is prohibited for most homeowner applications.

Finally, step four: Sit back, relax, and enjoy! Watch as your restored shore and natural yard flourish. With fewer yard chores, you'll have more time to enjoy your waterfront. You'll see more wildlife from butterflies to deer and everything in between. Perhaps the greatest enjoyment will come from knowing that your restoration efforts are helping to protect your lake or stream while providing natural beauty for you and others for generations to come. It's one of the best things you can do for our waters.

Note: County conservationists usually offer on-sight inspection at no charge or obligation. They'll suggest species to consider planting and sources for native plants and seeds. They will also answer your questions about funds available for your project.

Most herbicides and fertilizers cannot be used near wetlands or surface waters. *Permits are required before removing and/or transplanting aquatic plants in Wisconsin surface waters.* **Contact the DNR, your county LWCD, or Planning and Zoning Department.**

Up to 70% of the funding for your shoreland restoration project may be available through your county conservationist. This is a great opportunity to improve your waterfront and protect your lake. There's no better time than now to start your shoreland restoration project.

How big a buffer? Studies show that the greater the buffer, the better the protection it will offer the lake. The minimum recommendation for most waterfront properties is thirty feet, although fifty is better.

Want More Free Time at Your Lake?
Want to Protect Your Lake, too? Then …
Just Don't Mow!

While some shoreline property owners cringe at such a suggestion, the fact remains that putting your lawnmower away might be the easiest way to improve and protect your lake.

Far too much waterfront is landscaped to appear like urban yards featuring lush, sterile, manicured lawns. Shrubs and native plants are often removed by those new to our lakes and streams and replaced with a carpet of green all the way to the water's edge. The problem is that these manicured lawns have a serious, negative effect on water quality. Fertilizers, chemicals, and soils are easily washed into the water when rain falls on lawns. This often results in excess plant and algae growth, murky water, and fish kills. What's more, as natural vegetation is removed, conditions become ripe for shoreline erosion and loss of fish and wildlife habitat.

The remedy? *DO NOTHING! Just let it grow!* Let nature take it back. How much? The more the better! Join the *Just Don't Mow* Club! You'll be glad you did.

Reap the Benefits of Doing Nothing!
- *More time to enjoy your lake*
- *Reduced runoff and pollution*
- *Less algae and fewer unwanted aquatic plants*
- *Improved wildlife habitat*
- *More bird and animal sightings*
- *Reduced shoreline erosion*
- *Better fishing*
- *Enhanced beauty*
- *More privacy*
- *Respect from others who love the lake*
- *The satisfaction of knowing you are helping your lake*

Gain all of this just by reducing the area you mow near the lake. *Just Don't Mow!*

Left: This willow was planted one year before the photo was taken.

Below: These 12 to 20-foot willows vary between 10 and 15 years old and are due to be thinned to allow the balsam and red pine behind them to thrive.

Where There's a Willow There's a Way

The term, *shoreland restoration,* has been added to the list of buzzwords buzzing around most Wisconsin lakes and streams. Water education efforts by the DNR, the UW Extension-Lakes and others have helped folks understand the need for a natural waterfront. Most riparian owners now see the beauty and benefits of a natural buffer zone between the lake and their dwelling. Many have briefly set aside their fishing poles and paddles to take up shovels and hoes. Amateur lakeside landscapers are now replacing their labor-intensive, suburban-likes lawns with low maintenance areas of indigenous plants. Our shorelines are looking better and our lakes and streams are much healthier because of this effort.

Although some plants will take hold well and grow quickly, trees are not likely to show much progress for quite a while. If, like me, you are not a patient gardener, you may want to try the native willow to fill in those treeless areas along your shore. Willows are easy to plant, fast growing, attractive trees. Some can grow several feet in one season. This makes it possible to have a low cost, easy restoration project looking good almost overnight.

Start with a Plan

Consider which shrubs and other plants go where, thinking about sun and shade. Transplant your coniferous and deciduous trees according to your plan. Now, locate a large, healthy, native willow (such as Black Willow) in need of pruning. Take branches from ½ to 2 inches in diameter, 3 to 12 feet long. Back at the lake, remove ¾ of the branches and trim the cut end to expose fresh wood. Lay the willow sticks on the shore with the cut end in the water until ready to plant. Next, using an old ice spud or a pointed bar, poke some holes in the ground on shore at least two feet from the water. These holes should be deeper than the water level and spaced at least two feet apart. (Later you will thin them to four feet apart.) Insert one willow stick into each hole and tamp the surrounding soil firmly. The water in the hole will nourish the willows and they will root themselves over time.

Although some may lose leaves and might even appear to die, most or all will recover.

I first heard of this method from a dyed-in-the-wool duck hunter. He told me how he used to make duck blinds in his favorite marsh using this method.* Willow limbs stuck into the marsh bottom in a circle in the spring would grow into a wonderful, natural blind by fall. Since hearing of this method, I have succeeded in growing willows both near to and far from the lake. (*Note that recent laws prohibit planting in surface water.)

Planting Tips

- Plant your trees on shore, *never* in the water.
- Weeping willows, also called Chinese willows, are messy and not indigenous to Wisconsin. Use only native willows.
- If you plant away from the lake, keep your willows well watered. Water every day if possible.
- Rabbits and beaver might find your willows a tasty treat. Wrap the trees with poultry fencing to protect them. Deer are likely to browse on the young shoots of willows, too. Repellents or deer netting might help keep them at bay.
- When your other native trees gain their stature, you may wish to remove the willows to give the others the space they need to flourish.

This last step may be difficult. Some willows are too beautiful to remove. They lean gracefully over the water's edge, sheltering an abundance of life. Your willow stick might grow to be a magnificent, picturesque tree, providing habitat for birds, shoreline animals, insects, amphibians, and the fish that swim beneath its branches. Include willows in your shoreland restoration plan. You'll be pleased with the results.

Rain Gardens:
Surface Water Protection in Nine Simple Steps

One of the challenges faced by our surface waters is pollution washed from our yards by rain. Water flowing from lawns and hard, impervious surfaces such as rooftops and driveways carry chemicals, nutrients, and topsoil downhill. These alter the water quality when washed into our lakes and streams. Altered water quality can result in a change in the ecology of our waters—changes in the fishery and aquatic plant growth. These pollutants can even cause toxic algae blooms. Multiply such an event by the number of homes contributing runoff and the problem increases proportionately.

Rain gardens help solve this problem. They can save our waters while adding beauty to our yards. A rain garden catches the polluted runoff before it reaches the water's edge. As the excess water soaks into the soil below the garden, most of the pollutants are filtered out.

Rain gardens need not be expensive. If you plant self-naturalizing local perennials, the plants, shouldn't require much time-consuming weeding or other maintenance. Best of all, the garden will add beauty to your views of the lake or stream you are helping to protect.

The following is a simplified list of steps for creating a rain garden. It is based on information from various sources including the UW-Extension Learning Store publication, *Rain Gardens: A How-to Manual for Homeowners.*

This is a comprehensive guide available online at http://dnr.wi.gov/topic/shorelandzoning/documents/rgmanual.pdf. Printed copies of this publication are available from your county's UW-Extension office.

Creating Your Rain Garden

1. Determine the best location

To prevent flooding in your basement, place the garden at least ten feet away from your home. Twenty or more is better. Never locate the garden over a septic field. Avoid trees, as the roots might be affected by both your digging and the occasional filling of your garden after a rain. Try to choose a sunny, naturally occurring low spot in your yard where your downspouts can direct rainwater toward your garden.

2. Create a design

Determine the correct size of your project using the formula found in *Rain Gardens: A How-to Manual for Homeowners,* page 6. (See page 81.) Whether large or small, first plan your garden on paper to help create the best appearance possible.

Design your garden to be attractive from both inside and outside your home and from various places in your yard. How will it look to the neighbors? Consider enhancing the rain garden by using local or existing stone, ornamental fences, or garden benches.

3. Choose your plants

Native plants are recommended for rain garden installations because they are best adapted for local climates. Choose flowers and grasses that grow well in both wet and dry areas because the rain garden will temporarily fill with water from time to time. Consider transplanting perennials already growing on your property. They are already adapted to your yard and can help reduce the cost of your project. Many local greenhouses, garden supply stores, and local landscapers can provide advice on which plants will grow best in your region. A comprehensive list can be found beginning on page 18 of the UW-Ex Rain Garden publication referenced above.

3. Lay out the garden

Using wooden stakes and string, lay out the boundary of the garden. Then call Digger's Hotline (811), a free service that will locate underground utilities. (Important!)

First, Do No Harm

The first attempt at solving the problem of runoff toward a lake or river should be to reduce the size of the impervious surface at your home. Although this is easiest to accomplish when the home and landscape are being designed, it can also be accomplished years after construction ends. Whenever possible, downspouts should direct water *away* from the lake or stream. Parking areas and driveways can be sloped to direct water away, too. Pervious pavers can be used on driveways and walks to allow most of the rain to soak in rather than run off. Reducing impervious surfaces and constructing them with care can help save our waters.

4. Dig

After gathering tools and supplies, dig your garden approximately 4 to 8 inches deep. Use the removed turf grass and soil to build a berm along the edge. Be sure the berm is level on all sides. The bed of the garden should also be level. Next, prepare the soil by mixing in 2 to 3 inches of compost.

5. Plant

Following your design, place the plants about one foot apart from each other. Step back and look at the garden, then adjust the location of the plants as you like. Once you are satisfied with the layout, plant the flowers and grasses using a hand trowel or garden spade.

6. Mulch

Apply 2 to 3 inches of locally obtained wood chips, straw, leaves, or other mulch. This will help retain moisture and reduce weeding. (Because of the need to save rare, old-growth cypress trees in southern wetlands always avoid cypress wood-chip mulch.) Arrange your downspouts to direct water toward the garden if you haven't already.

7. Water, water, water.

Good watering will get your garden off to a good start. Water your garden every other day for two weeks or until your plants appear to be growing well on their own.

8. Enjoy!

Your rain garden will become a pleasant addition to your waterfront landscape. It should be especially pleasing when you see it filling after every rain and you know your effort is helping to protect our waters from polluting runoff.

Not Just for Waterfront Homes

We all live in one watershed or another. Across the nation, stormwater runoff is a main source of water pollution. As homes, businesses, roads, driveways, and parking lots are built, they cause rainwater to wash polluting chemicals downhill or into community sewer systems. Most of these pollutants eventually reach our lakes and rivers. Some end up in our groundwater. A rain garden in our yard, even though it may be far from any surface water, will help protect the waters downstream and the groundwater we all depend on every day.

But, What About Mosquitoes?

It's true, ponds foster mosquitoes. But a rain garden is not a pond and not intended to hold water long. Like a pond, it can create an attractive addition to your landscape. However, its primary purpose is to temporarily catch and hold excess runoff, then allow that water to soak into the ground, thus reducing the pollution of our surface waters. Although a rain garden may fill with several inches of water after a storm, the water will soon soak into the soil.

Unlike ponds, rain gardens do not foster mosquitoes because mosquito eggs need a minimum of one week to hatch. Water retention in your rain garden will likely be measured in hours. Bird baths, rain barrels, old tires left outside, and standing water in gutters and ditches are far more likely to foster mosquito hatches than a garden. In fact, rain gardens often attract dragonflies. Dragonflies eat mosquitoes.

Want fewer mosquitoes? Create a rain garden!

Lakescaping for Wildlife & Water Quality
This is a great guide to shoreland restoration available at www.minnesotasbookstore.com. Learn how to landscape your waterfront property to prevent shoreline erosion, restore wildlife habitat, wildflowers, and clean water. This book will show you the way to design your area for increased enjoyment of your lakeside or riverside getaway.

Fish Sticks

No, we are not talking about the fish sticks that are breaded, deep-fried, and served in the school cafeteria. These fish sticks are intended to improve water quality in our lakes. How?

Over the past few decades, many of the fallen trees that lay in our lakes were removed by waterfront owners to improve their shoreline. In fact, the DNR once recommended removal of all trees fallen into the water. This reduced habitat for countless numbers of creatures from crayfish to dragonfly nymphs and resulted in loss of cover. Water quality and the fishery suffered.

The trend today is to leave fallen trees in the lake unless they obstruct navigation or spoil recreational use of the shore. Left in the lake, the trunks, limbs, branches, and twigs become home to many beneficial plants and animals—creatures once denied a place to thrive. Consequently, lakes having too few submerged trees are now being "retrofitted" by county land and water conservation departments and the DNR.

Unlike Mother Nature's practice of offering fallen trees along the shore as underwater habitat, the Fish Sticks program cuts hardwood trees far away from the shore. This is done during winter. The trees are then hauled onto the ice where they are securely staked to the lakebed. As spring temperatures melt the ice, the trees sink to the bottom.

"Waterfront owners on Bony Lake in southwest Bayfield County, in partnership with the county and the DNR, began a whole lake restoration project to move the shoreline on their lake toward a more natural appearance with a functioning near-shore eco-system," said the Bayfield County Land and Water Conservation Department (LWCD) conservationist. "An innovative part of this project was the installation of large diameter wood (whole trees and branches) for willing landowners. Our Fish Sticks program offered both financial and technical assistance to interested waterfront owners and provided more than 600 trees for our lakes.

"The trees are selected according to sound forest

management guidelines. They come from the landowners' properties or from nearby parcels. Installation is done on the ice. There is very little disturbance of the frozen ground in the uplands. They are attached to the shoreline or lakebed by steel rods or cables so they stay in place while they settle in for the next couple of hundred years. As the ecological importance of wood becomes better understood by waterfront owners, interest in the installation of Fish Sticks continues to increase. The addition of wood to the littoral zone (near shore area of a lake) is the *next best* conservation practice after the restoration of native vegetation ... along the shoreline."

Why Wood is Good

Historically, the natural state of a Wisconsin lake shore is either a wooded forest or a wetland edge. "After the glaciers receded 10,000 years ago, the newly formed lake shores were colonized by the adapting vegetation which climaxed in forests of mixed hardwoods and conifers," said the conservationist. "These forested shores continued to provide essential complex habitat through the perpetual process of trees falling into the water. This continuous recruitment of trees is common on all pristine water bodies. Insects, fish, amphibians, birds, and other animals evolved with this abundance of near shore wood. It is now essential to their life cycles."

He continued, "Wood in the near-shore areas of lakes continues to play a crucial role in the ecosystem. The forest-lake interface creates edge habitat on the shoreline. This forest and lake edge habitat, like all edge habitats, is home to a rich diversity of species in high concentrations. Research has shown that a single tree along the waterline could have as many as twenty-seven separate species rooted on it."

Aquatic animal life colonizes on the woody structure throughout the submerged "lifetime" of the tree, which can be as long as 1,000 years. Trees along the waterfront also protect the shoreline from wave erosion. Wood in the near shore areas creates a wide variety of food for the animals in the lake, too. The bottom of a tree lying in the water can be home to 75,000 invertebrates. While the invertebrates dine on the tree, small fish gather to feast on them. Larger fish seek out the small ones. Research demonstrates that panfish in lakes with significant woody habitat have growth rates up to three times that of fish in wood-free habitats. And, not only do studies show there are more fish along woody shorelines, but they show that the fish feed in these areas at rates seven times higher than along shorelines void of wood. Moreover, waterfowl and shore birds utilize the high protein diet of invertebrates and small fish that frequent these woody complexes.

Submerged trees provide essential cover to allow fish and other animals to successfully complete their lifecycles. Healthy populations of all living things must have the opportunity to be born, live, and successfully procreate. The nooks and crannies of wood complexes offer critters safety from predators while at the same time concentrating prey to make predators more efficient. Wood provides the only place where some species lay or attach their eggs. Quality habitat for spawning and nesting produces more young. More young provide more prey and the cycle continues in balance.

The Fish Sticks program uses forty to fifty-foot trees. These absorb the energy of both wind and powerboat-generated waves. Without trees, waves wash against the shore, eroding it and undermining the shoreline vegetation.

On remote, undeveloped lakes, the density of naturally occurring submerged trees often exceeds one tree for every five feet. On Bony Lake, the density of wood was one tree for every 150 feet. The Fish Sticks project increased this to an average of one tree for every 30 feet. Although this five-fold increase is still only 20% of the density found on undeveloped lakes, it has a positive affect on the health of the lake.

"Cost sharing is available for the Fish Sticks program," said the conservationist. "Several lake associations and conservation groups have received grants to assist in this water quality improvement effort. It's a tremendous opportunity for riparian landowners to improve the quality of their lakes through the addition of more wood to their shoreline."

Statewide, the Fish Sticks program has been used to place around 5,000 trees in nearly 40 lakes.

Permits are required prior to placing any tree in any Wisconsin lake. For more information on the Fish Sticks program, consult your regional DNR fisheries biologist or your county's LWCD. For fish sticks financial assistance, visit the healthy lakes grant program. (http://www.uwsp.edu/cnr-ap/UWEXLakes/Pages/healthylakes/default.aspx).

For detailed information and a list of resources, see http://dnr.wi.gov/topic/fishing/documents/outreach/FishSticksBestPractices.pdf.

Thank you to DNR fisheries biologist, Scott Toshner and conservationist, Butch Lobermeier for contributions to this article.

8
GET ORGANIZED

Pitch in!

The task of protecting and preserving a lake or stream may seem overwhelming, especially in light of ever-increasing numbers of people looking for their special place "up at the lake." And the number of boat registrations continues to climb, although the number of lakes and streams remains the same, putting even more recreational pressure on our waters. Add to this the steady increase in the size of watercraft, new forms of aquatic recreation, changes in climate, ever-spreading aquatic invasive species, and dozens more threats to the health of our waters. It soon becomes apparent that our desire to be close to nature, be on or near the water, threatens the lakes and streams we love.

But, just as groups of individuals can be a problem for our waters, they can also be the solution. Across Wisconsin and other states, lake associations have formed to address issues facing the waters and adjacent shorelands. Members share a direct connection to the lake and a common interest with their neighbors. Most lake associations place an emphasis on educating fellow lake users about ways to minimize negative impact on our waters. Many monitor water clarity, chemistry, and overall water quality. Some apply for grants to address water issues. Others may raise funds to hire boat landing monitors intent on keeping the lake free of invasive plants and animals. The list of activities in which lake associations engage is long. Among the few things they cannot do is make laws restricting waterfront owners and others who use the lake. They can, however, give each member an equal voice in the protection and preservation of the lake they cherish.

What you can do:

76. Join your local and countywide lake organization. Your support will strengthen their ability to protect your lake and your interests.

77. If your favorite lake has none, consider forming a lake association. Participation in your lake organization is your best opportunity to learn about and advocate for your favorite lake. Read the association's past newsletters, visit the website, and attend the meetings to familiarize yourself with issues and activities. (See "Dinosaurs" on page 184.)

78. Volunteer to serve on a committee or help with a project. This is a fine way to ease yourself into the task of protecting your lake through an organized effort.

79. Consider serving on the Board of Directors. Terms are usually short and the work is rewarding.

80. Attend the annual Northwest Wisconsin Lakes Conference, usually held in late June. It's a one-day symposium and regarded as the best summertime lake conference in the Midwest. Or take in one of the other regional summer lake conferences held in Wisconsin and Minnesota. These are fun, educational events designed to inspire, motivate, and bring you up to speed on regional issues affecting your lake.

81. Attend the annual Wisconsin Lakes Convention, held in late March, to learn of local, regional, and statewide lake issues. Whether you take in one day or all three, you will find this an inspiring event with interesting exhibits, activities, and eminent speakers. (See WisconsinLakes.org for all lake event dates, locations, and registration information.)

82. Encourage others on and off your favorite lake to attend these events and to support their local and countywide lakes and rivers associations as well as Wisconsin Lakes, the statewide citizen group that advocates lake conservation and education.

Lake associations are most effective when all views are represented, including yours. Never assume someone else will represent your views and values. Decisions affecting your lake and your property values are made by those who participate.

The Five Levels of Lake Management

There is a certain ranking when it comes to the management of our lakes. They range from organizations serving all lakes in North America all the way down to the individual lake homes that line our lakes. The five levels of lake management are listed below in order of the significance of their ability to preserve and protect our lakes.

The **North American Lakes Management Society** or **NALMS** serves all fifty states and the Canadian provinces. As its name implies, NALMS addresses issues affecting lakes in the northern half of the Western Hemisphere. Its members consist of educators, scientists, statewide and provincial lake associations, conservation organizations, and businesses concerned with protection of our lakes and streams. Headquartered in Madison, Wisconsin, NALMS offers opportunities to scientists to present research papers and projects at their annual conference. The NALMS International Symposium is their main event of the year, typically attracting an international audience of 500 or more. The event rotates throughout the northern hemisphere annually. Their publication, Lakeline Magazine, offers articles, reports, and white papers on many lake-related issues, as does their website, NALMS.org.

Statewide lake associations are the second level of lake management. Most states with concerns about the future of their lakes have a statewide lake association. **Wisconsin Lakes (WL)** is an example. According to its charter, WL is a statewide nonprofit organization dedicated to conserving, enhancing, and restoring Wisconsin's lakes by fostering responsible lake stewardship and by promoting effective, beneficial environmental public policy.

WL's membership includes individual lake associations and lake districts, lake-related businesses, scientists, educators, and individuals concerned about our lakes, rivers, and watersheds. Each spring, WL joins with the DNR and University Extension to offer an annual convention of lake associations, government agencies supporting our lakes, businesses, and volunteers. WL's quarterly newsletter, Lake Connection, and their website, WisconsinLakes.org, offer a variety of information about lake management and other lake-related ideas. They also have an outreach program to help waterfront owners better understand lakes and how to protect them.

"Countywides" are the third level of lake management organizations. Although not affiliated with nor supported by county governments, countywide lakes and rivers associations take on issues affecting lakes within their county borders. These citizen volunteer groups offer local lake associations the opportunity to share information with each other. They also engage the county board on issues needing their attention. Often, these countywides conduct workshops and other learning activities for waterfront owners and do other outreach projects. They also work with adjacent countywide lake organizations to protect lakes, streams, and watersheds on a regional level.

Most waterfront owners are familiar with the fourth level of lake management, **lake associations** and **lake districts.** These grassroots organizations rely on volunteers to share information, conduct meetings, and act in the best interest of the lake and its users. Most of Wisconsin's 585 lake associations are registered with the State Department as not-for-profit corporations. The 228 lake districts also qualify as non-profits. As such, both types are eligible for grants to conduct water quality studies, develop management plans to improve water quality, educate boaters, and address AIS issues. Most have a board of directors and hold an annual meeting where waterfront owners can learn about and discuss issues affecting the lake. Lake association and lake district members are encouraged to join these organizations' boards of directors.

The fifth level of lake management is **you—yes, you, the waterfront owner.** Although you might not think of yourself and your family as "lake managers," the truth is that you have control over what happens on your property. You determine whether or not to use phosphorus-based fertilizer. You decide how much runoff flows across you lawn and enters the lake. You choose how great a buffer zone you want between your home and the shore. You select your waterfront lighting. And these are only a few of the many choices made by thousands of individuals and families whose properties line our shores and whose decisions determine the future of our surface waters.

These are the five levels—the key entities responsible for management of our lakes—ranked in inverse order. *Inverse?* Yes. Countywide, statewide, and even continent-wide lake advocacy organizations may be extremely important to our waters, and lake associations and districts are crucial to lake protection of individual lakes. But without a doubt, the most important of the five are the individual waterfront owners. For they control how their property affects the lake—whether phosphorus-based fertilizers are used, how much runoff will flood the lake with nutrients, how deep and effective the buffer zone will be, and whether or not a hundred more best management practices will be observed. They are also the people most able to monitor the lake for changes and work with the DNR and others to address lake issues that arise.

Protection of your lake will result in protection of your water quality and your property value. Do your part to protect your lake and participate in your local lake association, for they

work to protect your lake, too. And urge the association board to support the countywide and statewide lake organizations, for they do the same.

All five levels of lake management are important. All address the issues our lakes face in their own way. Think of them as a team—your team—and you are the defense, continually safeguarding your lake. Combined, they are a force assuring that future visitors will enjoy clean, safe, healthy lakes.

The Wisconsin Lakes Partnership

Wisconsin's rich history and leadership in conservation are known nationwide and include the protection of our 15,081 lakes. Whether a one-acre pond or 137,708-acre Lake Winnebago, every Wisconsin lake is important. So are the plants and animals that live in and near the lake as well as the people who visit or live there. The task of protecting lakes is challenging. Wisconsin's success with this is due to a unique three-part alliance that brings science, education, and citizen volunteers together to care for our lakes.

The Wisconsin Lakes Partnership has enjoyed national recognition as a model of collaboration since it was formed in the early 1970s. It is comprised of three partners: the Department of Natural Resources (DNR), who provide technical expertise and regulatory authority; the UW-Extension Lakes Program (UWEX–Lakes), offering educational materials and programs; and Wisconsin Lakes (WL), who mobilize citizen volunteers, lake management organizations, and business partners to advocate for lakes. Each partner contributes to the effort to protect and preserve our lakes, streams, and watersheds.

For example, the Wisconsin DNR conducts studies and collects and analyzes data to better understand our surface waters. Based on painstaking research, the DNR works with the legislature to establish regulations intended to protect our waters.

UWEX–Lakes offers a wide variety of educational materials designed to improve our understanding of lakes and how to protect them. Their staff members are specialized in lake issues and available for questions regarding most aspects of lakes and lake living. Among their many outreach efforts, the UWEX–Lakes team coordinates the annual Wisconsin Lakes Convention. The planning committee for this illuminating and inspiring three-day event is comprised of DNR, UWEX–Lakes, and WL team members from across the state.

The third partner, Wisconsin Lakes, brings the strength of more than three hundred lake associations and lake districts to the table. This represents an abundance of expertise in lake issues from all types and sizes of lake organizations. WL's website offers a wide variety of information to address virtually every issue regarding lake protection. And WL offers another advantage. Because both the DNR and UWEX–Lakes staff are state employees, they cannot lobby the legislature on their own behalf. WL has the ability and skills needed to influence the legislature for the benefit of our surface waters.

The Wisconsin Lakes Partnership—a three-legged stool—solid and strong—willing to take on the task of protecting our lakes through collaboration, cooperation, and leadership.

George Meyer, Executive Director of the Wisconsin Wildlife Federation and former Wisconsin DNR Secretary, referred to WL as "the most influential water issues lobbying group in Wisconsin." In July, 1999, The Wisconsin Law Review said WL is a "growing, well-educated, and respected force within the state ... in a position to generate an informed and active citizen network on both a lake-by-lake and a statewide basis."

When Leaders Act: A Case Study

The Wisconsin legislature has set the gasoline tax at 30.9 cents per gallon to provide funds for improvement of roads and bridges. Boats travel on water, yet still pay the required gas tax when purchasing fuel. Several observant lake leaders saw this as an opportunity. Led by Attorney Bill O'Connor, they developed a strategy, took action, and convinced the legislature that gas tax collected for marine use should be used to improve lakes and streams rather than roads.

Their effort and the subsequent legislative action resulted in more than $6 million per year being available for lake management and education grants. It allowed the hiring of professional lake managers to coordinate lake improvement efforts and other professionals to enhance water education and boating safety. The funds are also used to improve boat landings, provide boat washing stations, and address the ever-growing problem of aquatic invasive species.

Without this citizen-volunteer effort, the "motorboat gas tax" fund would not exist, nor would the grants used by many lake associations, towns, cities, and schools for projects benefiting our surface waters. Many of the UWEX and DNR lake specialists we rely on and the programs defending our lakes today would not exist, were it not for these few advocates for clean, safe, healthy lakes.

The Wisconsin Lake Leaders Institute

In 1996, in a statewide effort to promote lake stewardship, the Wisconsin Lakes Partnership offered an in-depth, advanced lake education program to individuals interested in protecting our lakes. Funding for the program came from a DNR lake planning grant, contributions from lake organizations, and individual donations. Soon, nominations were accepted for enrollees in the first Wisconsin Lake Leaders Institute seminars. Since that first class of lake stewards convened, over 300 lake leaders have completed the course of study.

The Lake Leaders Institute curriculum is comprised of three weekends of seminars and workshops on limnology, conservation advocacy, and leadership skills related to surface waters. The $350 cost of the program includes lodging, meals, field trips, equipment, and materials for the three seminars. Grants and contributions from lake organizations often subsidize the registration fee and related costs.

Over the years, Lake Leaders Institute graduates have aided in the effort to protect our lakes and streams by applying their newly found knowledge in a variety of ways. Some have become active in local politics. Others have become lake association directors. A few have been elected to local and county boards. All have contributed in their own way to the quest for clean, safe, healthy waters.

According to a UWEX publication about the Lake Leaders Institute, participants in the program "learn in an atmosphere of openness, trust, friendship, and camaraderie. There are three seminars held during May, September, and October at retreat centers around the state with the opportunity to take field trips, enjoy natural beauty, exchange ideas, and develop friendships."
More information about the Wisconsin Lake Leaders Institute is available at:

http://www.uwsp.edu/cnr-ap/UWEXLakes/Pages/default.aspx

Join Wisconsin Lakes

Whether we boat, fish, swim, visit our lakes for their natural scenic beauty, or own waterfront property, our lakes are important to us all. Unfortunately, lakes face an increasing number of challenges like the threat of aquatic invasive species, changes in land use, water quality decline, stress on both wildlife and fish habitat, and conflicts over how people use our waters.

The quality of tomorrow's lakes depends on today's decisions. But many decisions that negatively affect your lake are made far from your shore. Headquartered in Madison, WL works on the state level, seeking solutions to the challenges faced by many lakes. WL also supports strong local protection efforts. The volunteers who serve on WL's Board of Directors come from lake organizations across Wisconsin to work for all of our lakes.

WISCONSIN LAKES

The only statewide organization working exclusively to safeguard Wisconsin's 15,081 lakes, WL works with lake groups, citizens, and the legislature to assure all future visitors will have the right to boat, fish, swim, and enjoy the natural scenic beauty and serenity of our extraordinary lakes.

Although WL offers individual and business memberships, it is lake associations and lake districts that are the backbone of WL's capacity to safeguard our lakes. They also benefit greatly from WL's work.

Still, in spite of WL memberships costing only pennies a day, some lake organizations have yet to show their support.

Visit WisconsinLakes.org, then consider WL's long list of benefits and accomplishments. Now imagine what Wisconsin Lakes could do with the support of *every* lake organization. Whether individual, business, or an organizational member, you can play a vital role in defending your lake and defining the future of all lakes across the state.

For more information, visit WisconsinLakes.org.

"We love our lakes—the serenity, the unique recreational enjoyment they offer, the memories we gain from our days by the shore.

"The fact remains, though, that the only reason our lakes are healthy today is because others before us have worked to protect them.

Much of this work has taken place at town and county board meetings and in the statehouse.

It always will."

9
You Can. You Should. You must!

All (Lake) Politics are Local

We love our lakes—the serenity, the unique recreational opportunities they offer, the memories we gain from our days by the shore. But in order to ensure that our lakes are not ruined by irresponsible development or bureaucratic negligence, there are times when we must put down our favorite fishing rod and take up the tool kit of the political advocate.

Many who come to our lakes and streams do so to get away, to relax, to recharge. We don't relish the thought of trading precious time at the lake for a struggle to safeguard it. The fact remains, though, that the only reason our lakes are healthy today is because others before us have worked to protect them. Much of this work has taken place at town and county board meetings and in the statehouse. It always will.

We've heard it before: *All politics are local.* This is especially true when it comes to conservation of our surface waters and the quality of our lake experience. Like it or not, political advocacy is a necessity if we hope to protect our waters.

What you can do:

83. You can communicate. Keep in touch with your local or countywide lake association to stay up to speed on issues facing our waters.

84. You can stay informed. Others working to address political issues can keep you aware of local, county, and state issues regarding lakes and streams. (Follow your countywide lake association and local lake association web pages. Request lake news updates and bulletins from Wisconsin Lakes, too.)

85. You can act. When called upon, send a brief email, a letter, or make a call to your town or county official or state legislator to voice your opinion on lake-related issues. Remember, they work for you and need to hear your opinion.

86. You can advocate. Encourage others who value healthy lakes to become politically aware and to take an active role in affecting positive change.

87. You can write. Submit op-ed letters to your local media on lake issues coming before your town and county board.

88. You can network with others working to conserve.

89. You can socialize. Get to know your public officials. They listen best to those they know best.

90. You should attend town planning commission meetings where you'll get beforehand knowledge of proposed developments.

91. You should frequent town board meetings. Offer your opinion on issues affecting our waters.

92. You can speak out at county zoning committee meetings when threatening lake-related issues arise.

93. You should monitor the agendas of your county land and water conservation, zoning, and AIS committees. Let them know your opinion on lake issues.

94. You can attend monthly county board meetings to

show your county supervisors that lake issues are important to the public.

95. You must support those public officials who demonstrate good conservation ethics.

96. You should seek out new candidates for local, county, and state government offices who pledge to protect the environment and conserve our surface waters.

97. You should work to elect those candidates by posting signs, knocking on doors, and spreading their word.

98. You can run for a seat on your town or county board where your opinion can determine the future of our shorelands.

99. You must vote! More than a right, it's your responsibility. And encourage others to vote, too. Convince them that their vote really does count.

100. You must teach your children well. They will inherit what we leave but must know how and why our lakes and streams must be protected. Like us, our children hold the future of the waters in their hands.

101. Never give up. Remember, we are but visitors—the lakes are here forever. Let your efforts to protect and preserve our lakes and streams be your legacy. After all, if not you, who?

One way to serve our waters and those who treasure them is by becoming a government leader. Running for a county or town office is a wonderful way to make your mark and affect change in your community. Although the following explains the process of running for a county board seat, most of the information applies to elected town, village, and city offices as well.

Taking the Lead:
Affecting Change by Running for Office

Every Wisconsin county is governed by a board of supervisors. These dedicated men and women come from different regions of the county. Every two years, counties hold elections to determine who will hold these seats. Any resident of the county over eighteen years of age is eligible to hold office.

There are many reasons to run. Perhaps you feel you have good ideas about how to manage some aspects of county business. Maybe you have specific expertise or a desire to make certain improvements. Maybe you're just fed up with the job being done by your present supervisor or you feel he's been in too long. Some candidates choose to run because they feel a need to do their part. There are also reasons not to run, such as having no more than one key issue you want to change. And if you're looking for an easy job with little responsibility and good pay, this isn't it.

The process

In Wisconsin, elections take place on the first Tuesday of April in even years. If you choose to run, you will begin by declaring your candidacy prior to Election Day and completing form EB-1 (Election Board - 1), available from any town office or the County Clerk. Form EB-1 is also available online at http://elections.state.wi.us. It is important to declare your candidacy well before the year of the election. October or November are common, though some candidates wait until early December.

You will need to get signatures from a minimum of twenty county residents who support your candidacy. More are better, in

All this declaring and collecting and submitting puts your name on the ballot, a definite benefit. But you also have the option of running as a "write-in" candidate. No form needs to be filed but your name won't appear on the ballot. One advantage of the write-in option is that you can wait until the last few days before the election to announce, post signs, and campaign. This surprise attack technique has upset many elections.

case one or two are disqualified. Thirty is better than twenty when it comes to signatures. Submit the list to the County Clerk within a day or two of January 1 of the election year.

Next comes the campaign. The amount of time and effort you put into this will depend on your opposition and your interest in winning. You'll find help available if you look for it. Some candidates enlist others to post road signs. Some place ads in papers. Others take time to appear at community events, knock on doors, and shake many hands. Some candidates do little campaigning, relying on their reputation. Each campaign is unique. Your interest in winning will determine the style of your campaign.

The election will take place on the first Tuesday in April. If you prevail, you will be asked to participate in a training and orientation meeting shortly after Election Day. There, you will spend some time on Robert's Rules of Order, open meeting laws, and other matters related to normal operating procedures of the board of supervisors. You will next be assigned to some committees. Committee assignments are made by the board chair, who tries to accommodate the wishes of the supervisors but also tries to balance each committee. Each supervisor sits on several committees. Some meet monthly, others only as needed.

Compensation for time and travel

In Wisconsin, county boards meet monthly, often in the evening. Generally, supervisors receive $75 for each regular board meeting attended. Committee meeting compensation is $50 as are "Special" and "working" meetings. Attendance at training sessions, approved education activities, and similar events that may help develop a supervisor's ability to conduct county business usually receives compensation. Mileage is paid at the current state reimbursement rate. Overnight travel expenses, though rare, are usually covered. The County Clerk will fill you in on all these details at your orientation meeting.

Perhaps the greatest compensation received by county supervisors is the satisfaction of being part of the process of managing the county and serving in the best interests of its citizens. This is a great chance for those who value our lakes and streams to be part of a governing body that protects them. It takes time and commitment but the decisions made are of great importance and the rewards are well worth the investment.

For more information, contact your county clerk or http://elections.state.wi.us.

Other opportunities to serve your community and your lake include the local planning commission, town board, zoning committee, board of appeals, or any of a number of county and town committees. Each offers the prospect to affect change for the better.

"The ultimate test of a person's conscience may be their willingness to sacrifice something today for future generations whose words of thanks will never be heard."   *Gaylord Nelson*

Wisconsin boating regulations now require all boats to travel at no greater than slow-no-wake speed when within 100 feet of another boat, a raft, dock, or shore of any lake or stream. The original version of this law did not include the word <u>shore</u> when it was drafted in the early 1950s. Average outboard motor size then was 4 horsepower. As motor size grew, so did interest in high-speed boating and water skiing. Wakes and wave action from faster boats caused the erosion of many shorelines. Propeller wash churned and roiled the plants and animals that rely on near shore waters. High speeds resulted in injuries and death when boaters came too close to shore. In 1998, an opportunity appeared to add a single word, <u>shore</u>, to the law. Twelve years later, the new law took effect. This is the story.

Birth of a Boating Safety Law

In 1997, a group of waterfront home developers were intent on relaxing the DNR permitting process required when lake homes are constructed. They lobbied then-Governor Tommy Thompson. Unable to do their bidding without suffering embarrassment, the governor announced he intended to call upon the public to help him "simplify" all DNR rules and regulations related to Wisconsin's waterways. The Wisconsin Conservation Congress (WCC) was asked to recommend simplifications in the fishing regulations and other citizen groups were appointed to make suggestions in other areas.

The Wisconsin Association of Lakes, now called Wisconsin Lakes (WL) was asked to suggest simplifications to the state boating regulations. As a WL board member representing northwest Wisconsin lake organizations at that time, I immediately volunteered to serve on the new, ad hoc boating regulations committee. We thoroughly scoured the boating regulation booklet, finding only a few laws that could be simplified. Our committee offered several proposals. I suggested only one—to eliminate the disparity between the speed requirements of boats and personal water craft (PWCs). Boats, then, were required to travel no faster than slow-no-wake (SNW) speed when within 100 feet of a dock, raft, buoyed swim area, or another boat. The PWC rule was the same, but twice that distance from shore. I saw this as the perfect opportunity to protect boaters, swimmers, and especially the near shore areas of most Wisconsin lakes and streams. My suggestion to create a similar 200-foot-from-shore no-wake buffer topped the list that went to Governor Thompson.

Six months later, we learned the news. Though the easing of the permitting process for builders was approved, not one of the Wisconsin Lakes recommendations was accepted. Knowing the politics involved, we were not surprised. Our ad hoc committee dissolved, but not my desire to see our near shore areas protected from high speed boating.

In order to garner support from sportsmen, I offered the concept as a resolution at the WCC Spring Hearings, receiving an overwhelming vote of support. The resolution later received approval at the WCC State Convention and went to a study committee. I met with them, explained the need for the law, and was delighted to hear it would move forward, but soon disappointed when I later learned it died on the table. WL support seemingly died with it.

Months later, a friend handed me a folder containing a Stevens Point Daily Journal clipping. The headline read, "Body of Missing Woman Found." It was the story of 22-year-old Gina Winters who, while out for the first boat ride of the year on Lake Nepco near Wisconsin Rapids, was knocked into the water by an overhanging tree limb. The sheriff estimated the boat was traveling about 25 miles an hour, 25 feet from shore. Gina would still be alive had the law been in place.

With my term as a Wisconsin Association of Lakes director nearing its end, I was approached by the WL Executive Committee to serve as Vice President. I accepted, knowing this could help keep my quest for the law alive. The following April, I again offered it as a resolution at the WCC Spring Hearings, this time holding up the Gina Winters headline for all to see. My resolution was approved at the hearings and later by the WCC delegation, though both at a snail's pace.

Now President of WL, I recall a long, January drive to Stevens Point where I met with the new WCC study committee. They were not easily convinced boating in our near shore areas should be slow. Some complained it would take them too long to reach their favorite fishing spot. Others doubted their props did much damage to the shallows. The key to winning them over was the newspaper headline. I argued the issue of safety, their grandchildren endangered by high-speed boats coming too near shore, of boaters drowning after striking a rock or a tree. Still, they would not approve. Rather than see my efforts fail, I suggested a compromise. I would cut my proposed 200-foot SNW buffer in half. The committee approved and moved it on. Before I left for my long drive home that night, Steve Oestreicher, WCC Chairman, gave me some advice. "Keep up the fight," he said, "and start looking for a legislator."

The following April, my proposed rule appeared in the WCC Spring Hearing booklet, receiving overwhelming statewide support. I was also elected to serve as a county delegate and member of the Wisconsin Conservation Congress. I knew this would help me make some connections within the WCC and with the Natural Resources Board. The Wisconsin Association of Lakes listed my 100-foot SNW law as their top-priority issue. I watched as it slowly gained traction. I also found a legislator interested in the idea, Senator Bob Jauch, representing the 25th District (retired 2015). He read my letters and saw the logic behind a no-wake buffer. He agreed to author a bill. We included an "opt-out" provision that would allow local governments to exclude sections of rivers regarded as thoroughfares and some lakes used for waterski shows and boat races. Senator Jauch found several co-sponsors and it seemed the bill was on the fast track. We knew it would be approved in the Democrat-controlled Senate. But when it reached the Assembly, Republican Committee Chairman, Scott Fitzgerald, failed to include it on the agenda, killing the bill.

Another year passed. An election added several Democrats to the mix. Representative Spencer Black now replaced Rep. Fitzgerald as Assembly Natural Resources Committee Chairman. Senator Jauch submitted the bill again. Now named Senate Bill 12, we began calling it the "Safe Lakes" bill. We waited and waited, then heard the news that SB-12 had been scheduled for a Senate Committee hearing. In one of the worst January snowstorms of the decade, my wife, Sybil, and I were off to Madison to testify on behalf of the bill. Other supporters included a University of Wisconsin limnologist, a colleague from a neighboring lake association, and a spokesperson from the Wisconsin Association of Lakes. Although several Republicans on the committee argued against it, the bill was approved and sent to the Assembly to await another hearing.

Then, at the 2009 Wisconsin Lakes Convention, I received a visit from a fellow WL director and close friend from Madison, Judge Charles Dykman. He and William O'Connor, a Madison attorney specializing in Wisconsin's surface water laws, had a concern. It seems Lakes Mendota, Monona, Wingra, and other Dane County waters already had a 200-foot-from-shore no-wake buffer. Our 100-foot "Safe Lakes" bill would cut that in half. Not only could they not support it, but their influence was key to its approval. We solved the problem with an amendment to the bill allowing county and local governments to exceed the buffer zone limit.

Three weeks later, I appeared before the Assembly Committee on Natural Resources along with Judge Dykman, Bill O'Connor, and my wife, the only ones who came to testify in favor. I was elated to see no opposition. The committee approved the amended bill one day later. Within a few days, it was approved by the full Assembly and Senate. It went to the Governor to await his signature.

Government never moves quickly. We waited again. And waited longer, wondering why Governor Jim Doyle delayed. Four, five, then six weeks later, we received the answer. A special event had been planned for the signing. I received an invitation from Governor Doyle to attend the signing of the bill into law at nearby Tatogatic Park. My wife and I looked on as the Governor signed the bill before handing his pen to me as a gift.

Spooner Advocate, photo.

In 2010, a full twelve years after Governor Tommy Thompson rejected my idea, the Wisconsin Boating Law booklet contained the new statewide law. I had one task left. I wrote an op-ed letter to the Stevens Point Daily Journal. In it, I explained how the law never would have been possible without that dreadful headline I held high, again and again. And how Gina Winter's drowning, though a horrible tragedy, served to save many others from injury and death, and would save lives well into the future. Several days later, I received a phone call from Gina's mother. She called to thank me for not giving up on the effort and for offering Gina's family some closure they never had. It was and is the most moving call I've ever experienced.

Since 2010, most boaters follow the new law. Citations have been issued to many who have not. Several lakes have opted out and several others have opted for no-wake buffers greater than 100 feet. Best of all, our lakes and streams are safer for people as well as the pets and the plants and animals that depend on the near-shore zone. The "Safe Lakes" law—Gina's law—is right for Wisconsin.

115

Unintended Consequences

In 2002, recognizing the rapid spread of Eurasian water milfoil and other invasives in Wisconsin, WL lobbyists urged the legislature to pass a law prohibiting the transport of Aquatic Invasive Species (AIS) on state roadways. Unconvinced of the need for such a regulation, the legislature dragged its feet.

Dissatisfied with the progress of the lawmakers, several northern Wisconsin countywide lake associations approached their respective county boards with the same request. Most counties refused, claiming it was a state issue. They were right. State law said only local governments and the state had the right to pass laws affecting all the lakes in any given county.

In June, 2004, officers of the Bayfield County Lakes Forum argued the issue before the Bayfield County Board of Supervisors and won Wisconsin's first ban on the transport of invasive aquatic plants and animals on all county roadways.

The BCLF lake leaders never suspected what would happen next. Within a month, two neighboring counties adopted the same language, prohibiting AIS transport. That was the good news. The bad? The Oneida County Board challenged Bayfield County's right to create such an ordinance, sending the issue to then Attorney General J. B. Van Hollen's desk for an opinion.

The decision came quickly. Van Hollen reinterpreted the state law, declaring lake ordinances were no longer only for towns and the state. Rather, a county also had the right to make a sweeping rule for all lakes within its borders. This ruling offered every Wisconsin county greater control of how their surface waters are regulated—an extraordinary unintended consequence of the original BCLF effort. (There's little doubt that several influential Dane County lobbyists had a hand in Van Hollen's decision, for all lakes in Dane County had previously enjoyed county regulation. Dane would have lost that control if the attorney general decided against Bayfield County.)

Within a month of the Van Hollen decision, several more northwestern Wisconsin countywide lake associations convinced their county boards to adopt the new Bayfield County law. They were hoping to make the northwest corner of the state a "no-transport island" where counties would work cooperatively to reduce AIS spread. The state legislature, perhaps embarrassed to see northwest Wisconsin doing the lawmakers work, approved a statewide law prohibiting AIS transport in the subsequent budget bill. (This, thanks to 25th District Senator Bob Jauch [now retired] of Bayfield County who wrote the budget bill item.)

Although the story could end here, it does not. The BCLF worked with Senator Jauch to further improve the law. Recognizing the penalty for violation of the no-transport law was a mere slap on the hand, we asked for a significant increase in the fine. And, because the no-transport law could only be enforced by game wardens, BCLF suggested a line be included in the ordinance that would give authority to all local, county, and state law enforcement officers to issue a citation to any driver whose boating equipment carried any aquatic plants on any local, county, or state roadway. Both suggestions were approved and are now part of Wisconsin's no-transport of aquatic plants and animals law.

What began as an effort to pass a county ordinance to protect county lakes and streams from AIS ended with a statewide lake and stream protection law. It also won for every county the ability to now regulate the use of its surface waters. Both are monumental, unintended consequences of the original efforts of volunteers passionate about caring for our waters.

Do you have a suggestion for a better lake or stream regulation? Any citizen can work with their state representative or senator to improve the way we use our waters. Your local lake association or countywide lake association is a good place to begin. And, although most bills proposed to the state legislature never make it through the process to become law, as you can see from this article, a good idea along with perseverance may result in far more than you can imagine.

Because of the Van Hollen decision, you could consider pitching your new lake law proposal to your county board. Although no county has used this new ability to create a countywide lake law since 2004, they have the right. Examples of rules they could apply to all county lakes include:

- a time-of-use ordinance for aggressive boating.
- an ordinance protecting small lakes from use of large outboards.
- county restrictions on fishing tournaments.
- an increase in the 100-foot from shore slow-no-wake law for lakes in your county. (All lakes within Dane County have a 200-foot from shore no-wake limit.)

Lakes, Streams, and the Conservation Congress

The Wisconsin Conservation Congress (WCC) consists of 360 elected delegates, five from each Wisconsin county. They solicit public input and, through a process of public hearings and meetings, they offer recommendations to the DNR's Natural Resource Board (NRB) on rules, regulations, and issues related to the use of Wisconsin's natural resources.

Individuals and organizations working to protect and preserve lakes and streams have had great success in working through the WCC. For example, when the Cable Lake Association in Bayfield County recognized a problem with anglers over-harvesting largemouth bass on the lake, the lake association turned to the WCC. With support from the county fish manager, the association submitted a resolution calling for a daily bag limit of only one largemouth bass with a minimum length of eighteen inches. The following year, the rule was in the Wisconsin fishing regulations booklet.

The process begins with two copies of a simple resolution. Paragraph one states the problem. Next comes a brief explanation or several bullet points on the issue. Finally, your suggested solution. The person who signs the resolution presents two copies at the WCC Annual Spring Hearings, held in April in every county. The resolution is read before the group. Discussion follows. A vote is taken. If the majority agrees, the resolution is forwarded to the proper WCC committee for study. If accepted, it goes before the entire body of 360 delegates for another vote. If approved, it is offered to the Natural Resources Board who makes the final recommendation to the DNR.

> **WCC delegates gather information from fellow citizens on key outdoor matters. Issues are offered for public approval at the WCC Spring Hearings on the first Monday of April in every Wisconsin county.**

Any Wisconsin resident can run for the post of Conservation Congress Delegate at the spring hearings. Terms are either two or three years. There is no pay other than the rich reward of knowing you are part of an influential body of peers who value our natural resources and are willing to work to protect them by affecting rules and regulations.

> **In 1934, after complaints that the hunting, fishing, and trapping rules lacked input from outdoorsmen, the Wisconsin Legislature passed a law requiring the election of five volunteer delegates to represent each county. These 360 delegates became an advisory group to the Natural Resources Board. Today, the WCC is a great avenue to affect positive change in the way we use our surface water resources.**

A Sample WCC Resolution

The problem: In our county, fireworks litter can be found floating around the lakes after the July 4th holiday and often other times of the year. It comes from individuals shooting fireworks over the lake.

The litter is unsightly and indicates that other, more toxic fireworks pollutants, such as perchlorates and heavy metals, are entering the lake.

The county sheriff's office says requests for the required permits to use fireworks are very rare. Something needs to be done to protect the lake and the wildlife within it from this fireworks problem.

The solution: All landings on all inhabited lakes in our county should post a sign informing the public of the state fireworks law and the penalty for using fireworks without a permit. Furthermore, the county should post a notice in the newspaper each summer warning people about the safety hazards of fireworks, their potential to litter and pollute lakes and streams, and the law about fireworks permits.

This Resolution is respectfully submitted April 1, 2020, by Tom Terrific, 0000 Nevermore Road, Sometown, Wisconsin, 54321.

Author's note: The following is from a "toolkit" I prepared for WL several years ago. It will help you organize your association. At BayfieldCountyLakes.org you will find more information and newsletter articles that may help with your decisions.

Starting a Lake Association

To begin ...

When you read "5 Simple Steps" below, you'll see how easy it is to form an association. You will also find a document prepared by the Terrene Institute, UWEX–Lakes, and the Bayfield County Lakes Forum titled "Model Bylaws for Lake Associations." It is a simple, fill-in-the-blank tool that will make the bylaw writing chore a breeze. You will also find a downloadable version at BadgerValley.com. Note that the model satisfies the requirements for qualifying for some DNR grants. For this reason, it may be best to follow the model closely.

Your first lake association budget

Although amounts vary, most lake associations ask for $20 to $30 annual dues per member. When determining the dues for your group, consider budgeting $1.50 per member per year for membership in Wisconsin Lakes. Also budget $2 per member per year for your countywide lake association. These will be two of the best investments your members will ever make on behalf of your lake and all Wisconsin lakes.

You probably should incorporate as a non-stock, non-profit corporation. This simple, low-cost step offers several advantages. Incorporating helps your group qualify for state grants. It also discourages legal action against the association because a non-stock corporation cannot be sued for more money than it has in its treasury. There is a one-time $35 filing fee and a $10 annual fee. You will need Form DFI/Corp102. You can access this file directly from the Wisconsin State Department at www.wdfi.org/corporations/forms.htm where you can download form 102. If you prefer, you can request the form directly from the Secretary of State by calling the Division of Corporate & Consumer Services at 608-261-7577. Incorporating as a non-stock, non-profit corporation is easy, inexpensive, and highly recommended for lake associations.

Many lake associations apply for 501(c)(3) status through the IRS. This exempts the association from income taxes and allows the association to receive contributions and raise funds in excess of $5,000. Small lake groups often skip this, anticipating no need due to the association's small annual budget and no requirement to file annual tax returns. Other groups postpone the decision until they see the need. If you feel your lake association might eventually seek a 501(c)(3) exemption, it is far easier to file the application when the association is first formed. Applying later will require in-depth review of your financial reports and account records, placing a heavy burden on your treasurer. In fact, upon deciding to apply, some long-chartered associations have found it easier to dissolve, then form again, incorporating under a new name. Again, if you believe your group will need a 501(c)(3), do it at the onset.

Wisconsin Lakes is also ready to help you form your association. You'll find some good information on the WL website (www.wisconsinlakes.org). Give Wisconsin Lakes a call at 1-800-542-LAKE (1-800-542-5253).

The Wisconsin Lakes Convention takes place each spring. Hosted by the Wisconsin Lakes Partnership (UWEX–Lakes, DNR, and Wisconsin Lakes) the event keeps lake leaders informed of new issues and opportunities regarding their lakes. Try to send someone to represent your group and collect information to be later delivered to your association's members. The multi-day event costs about $70 per day plus lodging and other travel expenses but is well worth the time and expense. Visit WisconsinLakes.org for agenda and registration forms, along with information about other lake conferences and events.

Elsewhere in this book, you will find articles written for lake associations that I prepared for <u>Lake Connections</u>, the Wisconsin Lakes newsletter. One of these, "Why Join WL," explains the enormous benefit we all receive when we unite to preserve and protect our lakes. Another article, "The 3 Rs of Volunteering," offers advice on how to recruit, retain, and reward volunteers. At BayfieldCountyLakes.org, you'll find a how-to article on publishing a lake association newsletter.

Any information you find within this book or at the Bayfield County Lake Forum website can be used in your lake association newsletter and/or on your lake association website. Please credit the author and mention this book if you use an excerpt or article from either the website or book.

So ... Why Do We Form Lake Associations?

Lake management organizations serve many functions. They promote communication between lake folks, help clarify the needs of the lake, assist the DNR and other government agencies in conservation, and promote water education. They give the lake community a strong, united voice in local government, promote environmentally sound policy, contribute to the community, and help all lake users understand the fragile nature of our waters. Associations offer lake folks a chance to volunteer, donate, or help protect their lake in other ways. Lake organizations can preserve the memory of the past as they help prepare for the future. In time, every lake will experience a challenge, perhaps even a crisis. Having your lake organization in place will give you a head start as you face the complex task of protecting your lake.

Across Wisconsin, many lake associations have grouped together to form countywide organizations. The Washburn County Lakes and Rivers Association (WCLRA), the Bayfield County Lakes Forum (BCLF), and the Vilas County Lakes and Rivers Association (VCLRA) are examples. There are some unique advantages to these organizations. Countywides aid in the sharing of ideas, successes, and solutions to lake issues. They eliminate the need for each lake association to "reinvent the wheel" each time they face an issue. Countywides often facilitate educational functions such as lake fairs, conferences, and similar events that may be more than a single lake association can take on. Countywides also have greater strength in numbers when advocating for surface water conservation issues at the county and state levels. For example, in 2004 the BCLF successfully lobbied the Bayfield County Board to approve the state's first ordinance prohibiting transport of aquatic plants. Soon, other northern Wisconsin counties followed suit. The State Legislature did the same and Wisconsin's statewide "no-transport" law was passed, protecting many lakes from invasive species. Similarly, the 100-foot no-wake law remained a top priority for BCLF even when all other supporting groups gave up on it. Without this countywide lake group's drive and persistence, the concept would never have found the statewide citizen support it achieved. In an effort to protect an extraordinary stream and its surrounding woodlands, the WCLRA succeeded in having the Totogatic River declared a Wisconsin Wild River by the governor in 2010, forever sparing it from development. These are but three examples of the strength of countywide lake associations and their ability to serve our waters and those who cherish them. I urge every lake association to join their countywide. If you don't have one, begin talks with neighboring lake groups to form one.

Similarly, when lake organizations group together on a statewide level, their combined strength can positively affect the future of our environment. WL represents Wisconsin's lake associations and lake districts. This well-organized citizen group has enjoyed many important legislative and educational successes. It is important for your lake association to join with the over-300 lake organizations in WL to help preserve and protect Wisconsin's healthy lake heritage.

In summary, lake associations are easy to organize and manage. They can influence lake-friendly local regulations and offer social opportunities. They allow waterfront owners to improve their communication with the local community and to be prepared when issues arise. They are often the grassroots advocacy alliance that forms the last line of defense for the lakes we cherish.

> "Never doubt that the work of a small group of thoughtful, committed citizens can change the world. Indeed, it's the only thing that ever has."
> **Margaret Mead (1901-1978)**

Starting a Lake Organization: 5 Simple Steps

It may sound like a big task. It really isn't. With the tools and advice available today, forming a lake association can be simple and rewarding. Here are the steps. Start with ...

1. **Informal discussions.** Talk it over with a few folks on your lake. Share the list of lake association advantages found within this section. If interest is there, set a time and date and arrange for your lake group's ...

2. **Exploratory meeting.** Invite everyone who may be interested. Provide snacks and beverages. Also invite a leader from a neighboring lake association, your UW Extension Agent, and a WL representative to offer technical advice. Pass a sign-up sheet to get contact information. Discuss issues facing your lake and the advantages of organizing. WL and UWEX can help. Poll your group. If still interested, ask for volunteers to set up the *charter meeting* and others to develop bylaws, two easy tasks. Choose dates for your charter meeting and your ...

3. **Bylaws Committee meeting.** Here you will choose a name for your group, draft bylaws using the "Model Bylaws for a Lake Association," a fill-in-the-blank process. (See page 148.) Download a copy of the model to save keyboard time. This two-hour meeting will take a group of three to six volunteers. Ask UWEX or WL to review your bylaws, then send copies to your members. You will present these bylaws for adoption at your ...

4. **Charter meeting.** Be sure to publicize this well. Invite everyone, including the local newspaper. Let everyone know that you will vote on bylaws and elect officers. Before the meeting, ask folks to sign a roster, including contact information. At the meeting, begin with bylaws approval. Once adopted, hold elections. Your leaders should immediately (a) form committees, (b) accept dues, (c) join your county lake organization and WL, (d) fill out a UWEX Lake List contact form and sign your articles of incorporation, (e) select dates for your first board of directors meeting, annual meeting, and social event. Finally, after you adjourn, you should ...

5. **Celebrate!** You have just taken the most important steps toward protecting and preserving your lake.

The Three Types of Lake Organizations

Informal Association: Easiest to organize. Good for getting to know each other, improving communication, sharing information, and establishing some guidelines for your lake. Also helpful in lobbying your town board to do positive things for the lake or area. No authority to make ordinances. No state grants available. Bylaws are optional. Meet when you feel you need to meet. Often organized to promote social events. Some folks will join, others will not.

Qualified Association: (Recommended.) This is a formal organization with bylaws, a regular meeting schedule (such as one annual meeting and two board meetings per year), officers, and other requirements. Anyone with property within one mile of the lake is allowed to join. (Don't let this throw you. It won't be a problem.) Annual dues must be no less than $10, no more than $50. No authority to make ordinances. Good for getting to know each other, improving communications, sharing information and establishing some guidelines for your lake. Also helpful in lobbying your town board to do positive things for the lake. This is the most common type of association. Some folks will join, others will not.

Lake District: More formal yet, with specific statutory requirements and reporting structure. This is because, according to Wisconsin Statute Chapter 33, lake districts have the power to: create ordinances; levy taxes; borrow money; sue or be sued; make contracts; accept gifts; buy, hold and sell property; apply for grants; undertake projects to enhance recreational uses and more. A lake district board must include at least one member of your local government board, often the town chairman. This board, with local government approval and following state rules, determines the boundaries of the district, usually including properties well beyond the perimeter of the lake. There is logic to this, as people living in the entire watershed learn more about the lake and their responsibility to protect it by protecting the watershed. They also share the cost of protecting the lake. There are no dues. Instead, each property in the district is assessed a nominal amount. This appears on the annual property tax bill and goes to the town treasurer who deposits it into a segregated account accessible only by the lake district. No membership drive is ever needed because all who reside or own property in the district are members.

Grants up to $500,000 to study the lake, develop a lake management plan, control aquatic invasive species, educate, protect, and improve the lake in a variety of ways are available to lake districts and qualified lake associations.

All three lake organizations help neighbors get to know each other, improve communications, share information, and establish some general guidelines for those who share the lake. They are also helpful when it comes to lobbying a town or county board. Additionally, participation in your countywide association and Wisconsin Lakes assures your members they will receive proper representation on county and state surface water issues. Whichever type of organization you choose, your lake will be better for it.

The False Economy of Avoiding Membership

Lake associations need members to be strong and effective. If yours is like most, three things happen:

First, responsible waterfront owners support the association, knowing this safeguards their interests even if they are not active members.

Second, of those who join, a few work hard to make it a success by standing for office, volunteering for special projects, maybe even attending town meetings or workshops about lakes or leadership.

Third, some folks simply don't join.

Unfortunately, this third group will sit back and watch while *their* well-being will be enhanced by the others who work to protect the lake. Unaware they risk their own lake interests, those who don't join will squirrel away a pittance in annual dues—a perfect example of penny-wise but pound-foolish.

Meanwhile, the lake association that works for them may not have the strength it needs—both in terms of memberships and financial resources—to do the best work for the lake and all who cherish it.

We know it is right to support the organization that works to protect our property values and our waters. Making a small annual contribution to your lake association may be the best investment you can make—an investment in water quality, an investment in safeguarding the worth of your property, and, ultimately, an investment in serenity—the serenity you'll enjoy when you gaze at your lake, knowing you are part of the organization watching over it.

Is Your Lake Organization
Penny-wise but Pound-foolish?

Just as waterfront owners and other lake users should support their local lake associations and lake districts, the same associations and districts need to support their parent organizations.

Your countywide lake group and Wisconsin Lakes, the statewide lake association, have been working for you and are working for you right now. Check out their websites. Look at their accomplishments. Then imagine all that has _not_ been achieved because some lake organizations have not shown them support. This, in spite of the fact that the cost per member is less than a penny per day.

Your group's membership can add strength to WL and your countywide lake association. Don't allow your organization to be penny-wise and pound-foolish. Your group's support can only bolster their ability to protect your lake and your best interests.

Contact your local lake organization's leaders today. Request that representatives of WL and your countywide lake association be invited to your group's next membership meeting to discuss how they help safeguard your lake and your property values.

We achieve our best results when we work together toward common goals. As Marshall McLuhan said, *"On spaceship Earth, there are no passengers. Everybody is a member of the crew."*

30 Ways for a Lake Organization
to Better Serve its Members

1. Post or publish notices of all meetings (required by law for lake districts).
2. Meet regularly at a public place (required for lake districts).
3. Have your Hospitality Committee provide snacks, maybe door prizes at big meetings.
4. Prepare a written agenda. Distribute it well in advance of the meeting so people know what to expect.
5. Start and end your meetings on time.
6. Conduct your meetings in a business-like way. Be fair, brief, and to the point. Save chit-chat for after the meeting.
7. As soon as possible after the meeting, provide members with draft minutes or an informal meeting summary.
8. Review your bylaws and mission statement annually.
9. Establish a regular communication tool such as a newsletter to inform others of the association's efforts, board actions, volunteer opportunities, upcoming events, and lake news.
10. Involve your lake's youth through water education activities and fun events. Consider inviting nearby lake organizations.
11. Establish a web page or a Facebook® page for your lake group. Update it frequently.
12. Establish a secure e-mail list for association updates.
13. Keep members informed of key lake and community issues.
14. Provide an officer/board orientation fact sheet that spells out director responsibilities, duties, and related information.
15. Create a "member skills inventory" file with interests, resources, and skills of members.
16. Form committees and delegate responsibilities to involve more members.
17. Develop new leadership by mentoring and training members.
18. Send members to the Wisconsin Lakes Convention, the Northwest Wisconsin Lakes Conference, and similar events.
19. Send out surveys to give members input opportunities and ownership in the association's efforts.
20. Join Wisconsin Lakes and your countywide lakes organization, if one exists.

21. Meet with other lake organizations with similar objectives or concerns.
22. Enroll members to receive *Lake Tides,* the free UWEX – Lakes newsletter.
23. Establish opportunities for volunteers to gain a sense of ownership. Consider simple, fun volunteer projects.
24. Recognize volunteers publicly and reward the work of members.
25. Honor volunteers with news releases and photos sent to the local press and posted online.
26. Invite local media to your meetings, activities, and events.
27. Plan both social and educational opportunities for members. Example: An ice cream social with guest speaker.
28. Develop a lake courtesy code to help all lake users understand your lake's needs.
29. Maintain an active, creative recruitment effort.
30. Work with your board and your volunteers to make it interesting, worth-while, and fun for everyone.

APPENDIX

134

Stopping the Invasion: A 21st Century Approach

Toward the end of the last century, Wisconsin's DNR recognized the severity of the spread of invasive species to our lakes and streams. DNR lake specialists encouraged lake associations to round up volunteers to monitor boat landings, hoping to intercept EWM and other invasives prior to boats being launched.

The idea of asking concerned citizens to stand guard at the landing seemed logical. Thousands of noble, generous volunteers were trained. Of those, hundreds spent lovely summer days at the landings looking for that one boater—the one carrying aquatic plants—that needle in a haystack. But the whole thing fizzled out because volunteers could not be counted on to be there when most needed—summertime Saturdays, Sundays, and holidays, dawn until dusk. Who could blame them? After all, while one or two volunteers sacrificed precious time working at the landing from early morning until late evening, most others on the lake did little or nothing to help.

Time for Plan B, a special AIS prevention grant offered by the DNR. Many lake associations and town governments used the grants to train and hire "official" boat landing monitors to supplement the few, remaining volunteers. Because these people were being paid, they could be scheduled to be at the landing during peak boating times. It worked. The paid monitors, along with a few volunteers, covered the landings when needed most. They greeted boaters, explained the problem with invasives, and encouraged tens of thousands of boaters to inspect their boating equipment. They even intercepted a few who had plants on their boats and plans to launch. Success? Well, yes—sort of.

Plan B, though much better than its predecessor, had a problem. Although many boat landings were monitored during weekend hours, the other 150 or so hours in a week went unattended. Invasives continued to spread. What to do? What to do? What to do?

Along came Eric Lindberg, the owner of a waterfront property in northwestern Wisconsin with Plan C—an invention he named I-LIDS. It's short for Internet Landing Installed Device Sensor. Looking something like R2D2's cousin, Eric's I-LIDS is a heavy-duty, solar powered, stainless steel, tamper-proof, twenty-first-century thing-a-ma-bob. When installed near the landing, it fills the void, watching for trailered boats when human landing monitors are not there.

When a boater approaches, a motion sensor triggers the camera. As it videotapes the boat trailer and license plate, it emits an audible reminder—a voice urging the boater to check for plants prior to launching.

Is an I-LIDS camera as good as a person with a friendly smile offering to help you check your boat and trailer? Not by a mile. But then, a person can't be there all week. I-LIDS can. The best approach is to have both included in the plan to monitor your boat landing.

These cameras are now showing up at many of the lakes across northern Wisconsin and Minnesota. They are stainless steel sentries waiting patiently for the next boater to show up with plants hanging from the trailer, anchor, or prop. The image they take is instantly uploaded via the Internet to a server that can be accessed by someone with a laptop or smart phone who is authorized to view the images from the comfort of a lounge chair on the deck overlooking the lake.

So, do these I-LIDS gizmos work? You bet your bait box they do. When boaters see the sign, hear the voice, then see the camera, they circle the boat, looking in and under and all around, hoping to not be taped with evidence a warden might use to write a citation. And, yes, citations have been issued based on I-LIDS videos. And, yes, they have held up in court. But more than a talking camera, the I-LIDS system is a deterrent. It gives boaters a gentle wake-up call to check for invasives prior to launching. Its effect on boaters is not unlike that of a patrol car parked along the highway slowing down speeder after speeder. Watching boaters launch and land at boat ramps with these cameras in place will convert any nay-saying skeptic. Yes, I-LIDS works—works like a 21st century charm.

For more information on the I-LIDS system, visit EnvironmentalSentry.com. <small>Photos by Environmental Sentry</small>

The 3 Rs
Recruiting, Retaining, and Rewarding Lake Volunteers

Wisconsin has a long history as a leader in the environmental sciences and protection of natural resources. For decades, Wisconsin's dedication to the preservation of nature, its outdoor education efforts, and aggressive conservation programs have served as models for neighboring states and provinces. Early on, the credit for this went to progressive leaders who recognized the importance and value of environmental protection. The list of names includes John Muir, Fighting Bob La Follette, Aldo Leopold, Christine Thomas, Gaylord Nelson, Sigurd Olson, and others. Their exemplary leadership resulted in a much longer list—a list of individuals they inspired who so love and respect Wisconsin's natural resources that they voluntarily work to protect and preserve them.

For instance, many of the recent strides toward the protection and preservation of Wisconsin's lakes and streams have been due to the work of such volunteers. In fact, the

Wisconsin DNR now relies on volunteers for much of their needed water quality monitoring, invasive plant removal, and boat landing monitoring efforts.

Lake volunteers construct fish cribs and loon nesting platforms. Some maintain lakeside parks. Others work to educate about the issues affecting our waters. They host conferences, workshops, and events intended to educate those who use our lakes and streams. Those who attend these events often share information they've learned with others. Volunteers work to strengthen county shoreland zoning regulations. Some focus on educating young people about water conservation. In fact, many of our volunteers *are* young people! We have clean lakes advocates successfully influencing local, county, state, and national politics by writing op-ed letters, lobbying, attending meetings, and supporting environmentally friendly candidates. Grants have been awarded to volunteer groups intent on doing research to help lakes. Most of Wisconsin's boat landings have been improved by volunteer work. Thousands have taken on leadership roles in lake districts, associations, and similar organizations on the local and countywide levels. Because our volunteers monitor clarity and test water samples, Wisconsin can boast the strongest lake monitoring program on the planet. Our volunteer task list must also include the many folks who work behind the scenes on behalf of our lakes through statewide organizations, such as River Alliance of Wisconsin, the Wisconsin Wetlands Association, and Wisconsin Lakes. If we add all those who labor for our lakes in ways not mentioned above, we begin to see the immense size of the legion of volunteers protecting and preserving Wisconsin's precious waters.

Citizen organizations such as our regional and local lake associations often coordinate volunteer efforts. When faced with more projects than they have people, they strive to increase their volunteer ranks. Written for a Wisconsin Lakes Convention presentation, the following discussion suggests ways a lake association might attract and keep volunteers.

Recruiting Lake Volunteers

Inspiring people to donate their time and energy in order to protect the lake can be a challenge. Here are some key suggestions:

Get organized. Be able to explain what kind of work is needed, how much time it may take, who will participate, and similar details. Some folks are reluctant to dive in until they know where the rocks are.

Start small. Develop a list of rather simple, yet important tasks that can be done quickly by new recruits. Tasks such as affixing labels to newsletters or monitoring the landing sign may work for some lakes. For bigger projects, consider having several volunteers work together.

Throw a party. A group effort on a big project can become a fun social event. For example, a newsletter folding marathon can be turned into a party. Snacks and beverages are a must. Considering that the labor is free, they are a wise investment!

It's all in the family. Ask your active volunteers to recruit others from within their family. This is a great way to bring younger volunteers into the organization.

Spotlight the issues. Nothing brings people out to a lake meeting like a crisis. Although I would never suggest creating a crisis on your lake, it may be a worthwhile strategy to focus on a major issue or threat rather than taking a shotgun approach when recruiting. Once they're on board, and after the issue is addressed, your volunteers are likely to be willing to help with other projects.

Ask and you shall receive. There are people out there who are willing to help. Some will come forward on their own but many, perhaps most, will be content to stay in the shadows. You need to ask for volunteers to help care for your lake. Although a blanket call for volunteers in your newsletter may attract a few, person to person contact works best. A phone call or, better yet, a personal visit often instills a feeling of importance. People need to feel valued. Go ahead. Ask for their help. If you don't ask, you may never know.

Focus on their strengths. Some workers will do anything to help. Others, however, may participate only if they see a place for their specific skills. Once you identify the strengths or expertise of a member, explain the association's need for these skills and the value the volunteer could provide.

Do it for the lake. Make sure your potential volunteers understand they are not working for the organization as much as they are for the lake. Show them how it is in their best interest— in their lake's interest—to participate.

Show me the money. There are many reasons to protect a lake. A love of nature, a sentimental attachment, a wish to protect the resource for future generations, aesthetic appreciation, and a desire to have a healthy fishery are but a few. Some folks, though, may pitch in only if they see the financial benefit. According to studies done in New Hampshire, Minnesota, and Wisconsin, a one-foot change in water clarity can result in a seven percent increase (or decrease) in the resale value of a property. For most Wisconsin lake properties, this means twenty to fifty thousand dollars in property value. Although our natural resources are priceless, this gain in property value may convince some to volunteer.

Step out of the way. In some cases, potential volunteers may be reluctant to step forward if they see "veteran" volunteers covering all the bases. Having some of your veterans take on other tasks may give new volunteers a chance to rise to the occasion. Inform and enlist your veterans of this recruitment strategy so you don't run the risk of losing them in the process.

Offer free training. As mentioned earlier, nothing inspires volunteerism and commitment for your lake like sending a potential volunteer to one of the regional conferences or to the Wisconsin Lakes Convention. It's the best investment your group can make. Information on upcoming conferences is usually available at WisconsinLakes.org.

Retaining Your Lake Volunteers

The task of retaining volunteers is one of the many challenges shared by all lake organizations. Here are a few tips that may keep them on board:

Communicate. Keep everyone informed. Be sure your volunteers have the opportunity to participate by keeping them up to date on your lake projects and programs. Newsletter articles, Facebook entries, and person-to-person calls should be considered.

Level the field. All volunteers must be treated as equals. Treat people fairly and they will stay. This includes your association leaders. Leadership skills are important, but no more important than the many other skills your entire team possesses.

Never ask a limnologist to bake a quiche. Continue to focus on your volunteers' strengths and interests. Match tasks with workers. Let people do what they do best. Every lake organization has a wealth of skill and experience within its membership. Utilize these qualities to your lake's advantage.

Don't take your volunteers for granted. Keep in mind that they have other ways to spend their time. They are there because they want to be. If you treat them like subordinates, insult, or ignore them, they may not return. Others they know may not return as well. Sometimes this requires donning kid gloves, but the benefit of having the strongest group of volunteers possible is the reward.

Pay the freight. In certain cases, some volunteers may deserve a stipend for their work when that work requires an exceptional contribution of their time or skills. Some of the speakers we enjoy at conferences, a few consultants, and even some of the students keeping invasive plants from entering through our boat landings are paid stipends, even though they are essentially volunteering. Be sure to treat them as you would any other volunteers on your team. And, whether paid or not, *never* treat a volunteer as you would an employee. It is a sure ticket to the failure of your volunteer program.

No down payment. *Never* ask a volunteer to pay for the "privilege" of helping. Telling a potential worker that he or she must shell out money in order to be part of the team is likely to turn off some of your best potential volunteers. Although there is no harm in offering opportunities to contribute, it should *never* be required.

Listen up. Nothing turns off creativity and stifles enthusiasm faster than ignoring the input of team members. Leaders should lead by soliciting ideas from all, then working together to glean the best plans and processes. Offer every participant a voice. Suggestions should be encouraged at each turn in the road.

Rewarding Your Lake Volunteers
It is essential to show appreciation for the work your volunteers do. Here are a few ideas:

Let them eat cake. Seize every opportunity to say thank you, especially if it can be said in front of others at meetings or other functions. Arrange a banquet, luncheon, or afternoon tea where certificates of appreciation can be awarded. Invite the press, too.

Free and easy. When possible, offer your volunteers free promotional items such as hats and shirts bearing the logo of your lake group. Consider paying for their lunch when working on a project or event. Consider free admission to a conference or lake event. Such investments may help make volunteers aware that they are appreciated and considered key to the success of the project or the organization.

Media matters. Thank your workers in a news item in the local paper, your lake newsletter, or web page. Some folks like to see their names in print. It's also good PR for your lake group. The local press is usually pleased to get the news item.

Hand it over. Give out award certificates at your meetings and events. Consider giving a token of appreciation for outstanding volunteerism such as a gift card. Be careful about rewarding some volunteers more than others, though. Offering one, large award to an individual may deny others due recognition. If uncertain, consider hosting a volunteer appreciation party instead. Then, invite them all.

"Member" them. Some organizations award complimentary memberships to new volunteers and/or contributors who are not already members. In this way, you can honor them for their work as you recruit them into your organization.

The Wisconsin Lakes Stewardship Awards, a statewide recognition program, offers another opportunity to reward volunteers. Anyone can be nominated, an honor in itself. Each spring, one Wisconsin volunteer is chosen to receive the award, a plaque, and a certificate signed by the Governor. You'll find the process at WisconsinLakes.org along with more tips on managing your lake organization.

The 3 Rs, recruiting, retaining, and rewarding volunteers, can help your group prosper while improving workers' self-esteem, sense of place, and confidence in your organization. At the same time, the 3 Rs will bolster the impact of Wisconsin's thousands of volunteers who contribute time and energy in our never ending quest for clean, safe, healthy lakes and streams.

146

Blame the DNR!

Keep an ear out in any Wisconsin tavern or post office and sooner or later you're bound to hear someone cursing the Wisconsin Department of Natural Resources. And, why not? After all, each of us must comply with a myriad of rules and regulations crafted, some say, to prevent the public from making full use of our natural resources while enriching the state. So, why not blame the DNR when we find license fees raised or a forest road gate closed or a more restrictive daily bag limit when fishing certain lakes or streams? Why not point to the DNR when we are told we can't mow down to the lake, build a boathouse or a lakeside gazebo, or place a mercury-vapor light near our dock?

Deer hunters are told the wolf population is not a problem, yet they report seeing fewer deer than in years past. Blame the DNR. Duck hunters can't use lead shot. Blame the DNR. Boaters are told they must go slow near shore. They blame the DNR. Anglers are told how many fish they can take, how long they must be, how many lines they can have, what baits they can or cannot use, and on and on. Blame the DNR. Trappers, berry pickers, cranberry growers, wild rice gatherers, farmers, almost all of us face restrictions affecting our enjoyment of the outdoors. But ... blame the DNR?

Like our neighboring states and provinces, the harvest of our natural resources began when Native Americans gathered fish, mammals, and other food to live. Their impact was minimal—negligible compared to that of the Europeans who came here much later. Focused on becoming wealthy, French and English fur traders applied their business expertise and enrolled Native Americans in the harvest of mammals for the fur trade. They swapped traps, muskets, blankets, pots, beads, and similar goods for the precious pelts of beaver, mink, fox, and other mammals. With no government regulation on the harvest of game, the fur companies took all they could. This led to the decline of several species, most notably the beaver, prized in Western Europe for use in making gentlemen's beaver felt top hats. By the mid-1800s, the once abundant beaver all but disappeared. Without regulation, their population did not recover until the following century.

Other than scattered Native American villages and the occasional fur trader, northern Wisconsin saw little settlement until the great white pine harvest of the 1880s when several hundred thousand lumberjacks arrived. Railroads soon crisscrossed the state. Boom towns sprang up. A mix of sportsmen and market hunters arrived to take advantage of the new wilderness and its fish and game opportunities. Deer, bear, and waterfowl were packed in ice and shipped on rail cars to restaurants and meat packing companies down south. So, too, trout, panfish, and game fish. With no bag limits or restrictions on methods used to harvest these resources, their numbers quickly diminished. The land suffered as well. Brush quickly covered the north where the pine once stood. During droughts, the dry white pine treetops, limbs, and brush fueled enormous forest fires. Rains then washed ash and topsoil into our lakes and streams, exhausting forestlands and damaging fisheries for decades.

With Wisconsin's once abundant fish and game populations rapidly declining, people who had relied on harvesting deer, waterfowl, and fish to survive found it increasingly difficult. But it wasn't until the obliteration of North America's most abundant bird, the passenger pigeon, that the Wisconsin legislature took notice of the need for strict regulation. *Pigeoners*, a name given to professionals who killed passenger pigeons for restaurants and meat markets, had systematically killed off many millions of these dove-like creatures—birds once so great in number that the sky would be darkened for hours when a flock flew over. With no bag limit and no restrictions on the type of guns and nets used, the pigeoners harvested them by the hundreds, even thousands per day. The last passenger pigeon died in 1914 at the Cincinnati Zoo, and the species was extinct.

In 1927, responding to the rapid decline in fish and game populations and the devastation from forest fires, the legislature established the Wisconsin Conservation Commission, the predecessor of today's DNR. Decades after statehood, commissioners finally began a list of rules, regulations, and limitations for those who harvested fish and game for their livelihood and those who did so for sport. The University of Wisconsin established its own Department of Agriculture and initiated programs designed to improve farming and the timber trade. Based on recommendations from UW scientists, the legislature developed Conservation Department regulations to improve these industries. Wisconsin soon led the nation in conservation efforts, an honor held for the next eight decades. Yet something was amiss. Legislators had been making the rules and regulations governing how our natural resources would and would not be used. The public had been left out of the decision-making process. The public demanded a voice.

In 1934, responding to pleas from sportsmen and women across the state for greater rule-making input, the State Legislature established the Wisconsin Conservation Congress (WCC). This citizen-based group of advisors would offer recommendations to the lawmakers and the Conservation Department. Each of our 72 counties elected five Conservation Congress delegates to convene locally, then meet at an annual statewide convention to recommend improvements in the management of our natural resources.

After hearing the recommendations offered by the WCC delegates, a Natural Resources Board, consisting of seven governor-appointed citizens from across the state, assisted in the rule-making process. People now had a voice regarding conservation-related rules and regulations—the only state in the nation to offer such a progressive policy to its citizens.

Today, over eight decades after the establishment of the

149

Wisconsin Conservation Congress, any citizen of the state can stand for election as a delegate and have a say in DNR rules and regulations. Further, *anyone* can submit a resolution suggesting a change in these rules and regulations and know that fellow citizens will act on it. Many of the recommendations offered at the annual Spring Conservation Congress Hearings—held in every county and open to the public—eventually find their way to the Natural Resources Board, the DNR, and our legislators. In addition, your WCC delegates are waiting to hear from you, waiting to hear what improvements *you* suggest for the future health and use of our natural resources.

Blame the DNR? Sure. If it makes you feel better, go ahead. But keep in mind that the rules and regulations we all must follow have been crafted not in some smoke-filled back room by an anonymous, monolithic ministry working to make your life miserable. Instead, in Wisconsin, the rules affecting how we use our natural resources are made *for* us and *by* us— we, your neighbors—and you. Yes, you—if you have the pluck.

Even though Wisconsin established statehood in 1848, the first realization of a need for government regulation of our natural resources did not occur until after the turn of the 20th century when Wisconsin's Conservation Department was formed. Even then, a lifetime "Sportsman's" license (allowing the taking of most fish and game species) cost only a quarter. The daily bag limit on trout was set at 50, not the three or five of today. Most other fish and game bag limits were also high compared to today's regulations.

Model Bylaws for a Lake Association

This is a basic template for lake association bylaws originally drafted by the Terrene Institute and later modified by UWEX–Lakes, then by the Bayfield County Lakes Forum. Using this model, the task of writing lake association bylaws is simple. As written, they meet the DNR requirements for becoming a Qualified Lake Association, enabling application for DNR lake grants. Prior to adoption, submit your final draft to your DNR lake management specialist for review.

BYLAWS
ANYLAKE LAKE ASSOCIATION, INC.
P.O. BOX _____, _____ _____(1)

Article I - PURPOSE

The purpose of the Association is to preserve and protect Anylake and its surroundings, and to enhance the water quality, fishery, boating safety, and aesthetic values of Anylake, as a public recreational facility for today and for future generations.(2)

Article II - STATUTES AND LIMITATIONS

To carry out the program of the Association and to make effective representations on behalf of its members, the Association shall be organized as a non-profit, non-stock corporation under Chapter 181 of the Wisconsin Statutes. (Sections of the Statutes are cited throughout these bylaws.) No asset of the association shall benefit any officer or member. The Association shall not participate in partisan political activity.

Article III - MEMBERSHIP

Section 1 - ELIGIBILITY: Membership shall be open to any individual, family, business, or organization that (a) subscribes to the purposes of the Association and (b) owns or leases property in the vicinity of the lake.(3)

Section 2 - DUES: Dues shall be $____ per year.(4)(5)

Article IV - VOTING

Section 1 - MULTIPLE VOTING: Any individual member may cast only one vote on any question called to a vote. Up to two individuals may represent a family, a business, or organization; and each of those two individuals may cast one vote on any question called to a vote.(6)

Section 2 - CASTING BALLOTS: A member must be present at the meeting at the time the vote is called in order to vote. No member may vote by proxy(7) or absentee ballots.(8) All votes shall be counted by a show of hands unless otherwise specified in these By-laws.

Section 3 - REFERENDA: The Board of Directors may at any time solicit reactions from members through a mail survey. The Board resolution authorizing the referendum shall indicate whether the results shall be considered advisory or binding on the Board. The annual meeting may initiate an advisory or a binding referendum and shall specify the exact wording of the question and the required follow-up action by the Board. Members shall have 30 days to return response forms. Results of the referendum shall be announced at a membership meeting or in printed form within 90 days of the response deadline.

Article V - MEMBERSHIP MEETINGS

Section 1 - ANNUAL MEETING: The annual meeting of the Association shall be held in the vicinity of _____ Lake on the (first, second, third, fourth) (day of week) of (month). The time and place shall be arranged by the Board of Directors unless specified by the previous annual meeting. The agenda of the annual meeting shall include elections, discussion of projects, adoption of a budget, member concerns, and an educational program. [Sec. 181.14(1)(2)]

Section 2 - SPECIAL MEETINGS: A special meeting of the Association may be called at any time by the President, by majority vote of the Board of Directors, or by written request of one-twentieth of the members or six members, whichever is greater. The agenda of a special meeting may include any items properly brought before an annual meeting. [Sec. 181.14(3)]

Section 3 - INFORMATIONAL MEETING OR SOCIAL EVENT: The Association may sponsor a variety of meetings and events designed to provide educational, recreational, or social opportunities for its members and their guests. It may also sponsor fund-raising activities. If business is to be conducted at such events, the notice requirement for special meetings must be met.

Section 4 - NOTIFICATION: Every annual or special meeting must be preceded by notice to paid members and members from the preceding year who have not yet renewed their membership. Notification may be by hand delivery or by mail at least 30 days, but not more than 50, prior to annual meetings and at least 15 days, but not more than 50, prior to special meetings. The notice shall summarize any proposed changes in the By-laws, shall highlight any proposals to dissolve the Association, and may include a detailed agenda. [Sec. 181.15]

Section 5 - QUORUM: No formal business may be conducted at membership meetings unless at least one-twentieth of the paid-up members or 15 members, whichever is less, are present.(9) [Sec. 181.17]

Section 6 - PROCEDURE: Roberts Rules of Order, in the current revised edition, shall be in force at the meetings of the Association, of the Board of Directors, and of the Association committees unless required otherwise by Wisconsin Statutes or these By-laws. Non-members of the Association may be recognized to speak at Association functions at the discretion of the presiding officer who shall also serve as parliamentarian.

Article VI - BOARD OF DIRECTORS
Section 1 - AUTHORITY: Subject to directives of annual and

special meetings and these By-laws, the Board of Directors shall have authority over the activities and assets of the Association.

Section 2 - COMPOSITION: The Board of Directors shall include the President, Vice-President, Secretary, Treasurer, four(10) at-large directors, and the past President. [Sec. 181.20(1)]

Section 3 - ELECTIONS: The Board of Directors shall nominate one or more members for each vacant position on the Board. Additional nominations of members, present at the annual meeting and willing to serve, shall be taken from the floor. All elections for the Board shall be conducted by secret, written ballot. [Sec. 181.20(2)]

Section 4 - TERMS OF OFFICE: Directors are elected for two-year terms. Their terms shall expire after the annual meeting or upon the election of new Directors, whichever occurs later. The terms of office of President, Vice-President, and two at-large directors expire in even-numbered years. The terms of office of Secretary, Treasurer, and two at-large directors expire in odd-numbered years. [Sec. 181.20(3)]

Section 5 - BOARD MEETINGS: The new Board shall meet within 60 days of the annual meeting and at least one other time prior to the next annual meeting. Regular meetings shall be held at places, dates, and times established by the Board. Special meetings may be held on the call of the President or any three Directors after at least 24 hours notice by telephone, mail, or personal contact. Four directors shall constitute a quorum for the transaction of business. The meetings shall be open to the members. Decisions shall be made by majority vote of directors present, with the President voting only to break ties. Between meetings, the President may solicit decisions from the Board through written communications. [Sec. 181.22; Sec. 181.24]

Section 6 - VACANCIES: Any director who misses two consecutive meetings without good cause as determined by the Board may, at the discretion of the Board, be removed from office. Any vacancy may be filled for the remainder of the term by the affirmative vote of a majority of the directors then in office, although less than a quorum but at least two. [Sec. 181.20(4); Sec. 181.21]

Section 7 - COMPENSATION: Directors shall not be compensated for their time and effort.(11) The Board may authorize officers, directors, and committee members to be paid actual and necessary expenses incurred while on Association business.

Article VII - OFFICERS
Section 1 - PRESIDENT: The President shall preside over all membership meetings and Board meetings. The President shall be the chief executive officer of the Association, responsible for day-to-day administration of the affairs of the Association and supervision of any employees or contractors. The President shall appoint all committee members who shall serve until the end of that President's term. The President is an ex-officio member of all committees.

Section 2 - VICE PRESIDENT: The Vice President shall assume the duties of the President should that office become vacant and shall preside at meetings when the President is unable to attend. The Vice President shall arrange for the educational segment of the annual meeting and carry out other assignments at the request of the President.

Section 3 - SECRETARY: The Secretary shall maintain the official records of the Association as well as an archive. The Secretary shall record and distribute the minutes of member meetings and Board meetings. The Secretary shall maintain a current record of the names and addresses of members entitled to vote and shall send out notices of membership meetings. The

Secretary shall prepare publicity for the Association and shall prepare the Association newsletter unless an editor is appointed to do so. The Secretary shall serve on the Membership Committee. [Sec. 181.27]

Section 4 - TREASURER: The Treasurer shall maintain the financial records of the Association and shall sign all checks. The Treasurer shall prepare an annual financial statement for the annual meeting and shall be responsible for presentation of the proposed budget to the annual meeting. The Treasurer shall serve on the Finance Committee.

Section 5 - MULTIPLE OFFICE HOLDING:(12) The same person may hold the offices of Vice President and Treasurer or the offices of Secretary and Treasurer. [Sec. 181.25(1)]

Section 6 - OTHER OFFICERS Other officers may be appointed by the President, with concurrence of the Board. A legal counsel, an executive secretary, newsletter editor, or such other assistant officers as are deemed necessary need not be members of the Association.

Article VIII - COMMITTEES
Section 1 - MEMBERSHIP COMMITTEE: The Membership Committee shall initiate plans for recruiting of new members and retention of members.

Section 2 - SOCIAL COMMITTEE: The Hospitality Committee shall provide refreshments at the Annual Meeting and, after receiving Board approval, shall organize and publicize other social events to be sponsored by the Association.

Section 3 - FINANCE COMMITTEE: The Finance Committee shall recommend fund-raising activities to the Board and, after receiving Board approval, shall organize such activities. The Finance Committee shall also annually audit the financial records of the Association.

Section 4 - LAND USE COMMITTEE: The Land Use Committee shall represent the Association at local public hearings and informational meetings relating to zoning, sanitation codes, subdivision ordinances, pollution sources, and changes in land use which might affect water quality. The Committee shall offer proposals to the Board regarding land use issues.

Section 5 - BOATING SAFETY COMMITTEE: The Boating Safety Committee shall represent the Association at local public hearings and informational meetings relating to water safety patrols, lake use ordinances, and obstacles to navigation. The Committee shall offer proposals to the Board regarding water use issues.

Section 6 - FISHING AND WATER QUALITY COMMITTEE: The Fishing and Water Quality Committee shall represent the Association at Department of Natural Resources hearings and at local meetings relating to in-lake water quality, fish and wildlife habitat, and water levels. The Committee shall offer proposals to the Board regarding water quality monitoring and ecological management of the fishery.

Section 7 - AQUATIC PLANT AND ALGAE COMMITTEE: The Aquatic Plant and Algae Control Committee shall represent the Association at Department of Natural Resources hearings and at local meetings relating to the control of nuisance plants and to the protection of desirable vegetation. The Committee shall offer proposals to the Board for a vegetation management plan and may be delegated responsibility to implement such a plan.

Section 8 - OTHER COMMITTEES: The President may appoint such other committees as are deemed necessary to support the efforts of the Board.

Article IX - MISCELLANEOUS PROVISIONS
Section 1 - INDEMNIFICATION OF OFFICERS AND
DIRECTORS: As provided by Wisconsin law, the Association
shall indemnify any officer, director, employee, or agent who
was, is, or may be involved in legal proceedings by virtue of his
or her good faith actions on behalf of the Association. [Sec.
181.045](13)

Section 2 - FISCAL YEAR: The records and accounts of the
Association shall be maintained on a calendar year basis.

Section 3 - ACCOUNTS AND INVESTMENTS: Funds of the
Association shall be promptly deposited at a financial institution
designated by resolution of the Board of Directors. Funds not
needed for current operations shall be deposited in investment
accounts or certificates as authorized by the Board of Directors.

Article X - ADOPTION AND AMENDMENTS
These By-laws, and any amendments thereto, may be adopted at
any annual or special meeting of the Association by two-thirds
vote of members present and entitled to vote. Proposed
amendments to the By-laws must be summarized in the notice
for the subsequent annual meeting.

Article XI - DISSOLUTION
The Board of Directors, by a two-thirds affirmative vote of all
directors, may recommend that the Association be dissolved and
that the question of such dissolution be submitted to a vote at a
subsequent meeting of members. Notice of the meeting shall
highlight the question of dissolution. At the meeting, a two-
thirds affirmative vote of members present and entitled to vote
shall be required to approve a resolution of dissolution. Such
action shall direct the Board to prepare a dissolution plan for
subsequent approval by the members as provided under
Wisconsin law. Dissolution shall not be final until the members,
by majority vote, have approved the dissolution. [Sec. 181.50;
Sec. 181.52]

CERTIFICATION

These By-laws were adopted by vote of _____yes and _____no at the Association meeting on this _____ day of _____, 20__.

_____
Secretary

(1) If practical, the Association should have a permanent post office box to facilitate contact with members and other organizations.

(2) To quality for tax exemption under Sec. 501(c)(3) of the Internal Revenue Code, the benefits of a nonprofit organization's activities must flow principally to the public (but the membership can, of course, share fully in those benefits). If exemption under Sec. 501(c)(3) is to be pursued, the purpose statement must stress public benefits before, but not necessarily excluding, membership benefits. [IRS Revenue Ruling 70-186, Lake Association Tax Exemption]

(3) If people or organizations that do not own property are invited to join the Association, the last phrase (b) can be deleted. To be a qualified lake association, membership must be open to any individual who resides within 1 mile of the lake at least 1 month each year or any individual who owns real estate within 1 mile of the lake.

(4) This figure can be set at any amount agreed to by the members. However, we recommend that the dues be part of the By-laws to give them stability. Many associations discuss the dues at every annual business meeting. Frequent discussion of dues not only wastes time, but focus energy on an inherently unpleasant aspect of the organization. To be a qualified lake association, dues for voting membership must not be less than $10 or more than $50 per year.

(5) Sec. 181.12(2) Wisconsin Statutes requires agreement by two-thirds of all members eligible to vote to expel a member. If the Association wants an explicit policy, add the following to Article II:

"Section 3 - TERMINATION OF MEMBERSHIP: A member may be expelled from the Association for cause, on a two-thirds affirmative vote of all members present. They are entitled to vote at a membership meeting, provided that the matter shall have been included in notice of the meeting, and provided that the member to be expelled shall have been formally notified in writing at least 30 days prior to the meeting, and given the opportunity to appear and speak on his/her behalf at the meeting prior to the final vote. The motion shall specify the duration of the expulsion, not to exceed five years. [Sec. 181.12(2)]"

(6) The number of votes for families, businesses, or organizations could be limited to one per membership. Two votes are suggested because of the prevalence of husband and wife ownership of lake property.

(7) Proxy voting is not recommended because it tends to disrupt the egalitarian nature of association meetings. However, proxy voting is legal. [Sec. 181.16(2)] To provide for proxy voting, substitute the following for Article III Section 2 in the Model:

"Section 2 - CASTING BALLOTS: A member may vote in person at meetings of the Association or may vote by providing a written proxy to another person. A copy of the proxy must be presented to the presiding officer prior to the convening of the meeting. The presiding officer shall announce that proxy notices have been received and may ask each proxy holder to identify the member on whose behalf the votes are being cast. All votes shall be counted by a show of hands unless otherwise specified in the By-laws."

160

(8) Absentee voting is not recommended because many associations allow nominations from the floor and because many associations are not prepared to provide official ballots prior to the meeting. However, elections may be conducted by mail and absentee voting is not prohibited. [Sec. 181.16(2)] To provide for absentee voting, substitute the following for Article III Section 2 in the model:

Section 2 - CASTING BALLOTS: Votes for Board of Directors may be cast in person or by absentee ballot. To participate in other votes, a member must be present at the time the vote is called. No member may vote by proxy. Votes shall be counted by a show of hands unless otherwise specified in the By-laws.

Members wishing to vote for the Board by absentee ballot must request a ballot from the Secretary at least 10 days prior to the annual meeting. The ballot shall be returned in a sealed envelope clearly marked 'BALLOT,' shall contain the name of the member on the outside of the envelope, and shall be opened after the ballots are cast at the annual meeting."

(9) The quorum number can be altered. However, restrictive quorums are not recommended. The people who are asked to go back home from a poorly attended meeting are less likely to attend a rescheduled meeting. The attendance at the rescheduled meeting may be even poorer.

(10) A large association might want six at-large directors. In special circumstances, an association may want to ensure that one or two of the directors own property in a certain area. For example, in an association dominated by Big Star Lake but including Little Star Lake, two of the directorships might be reserved for Little Star Lake property owners.

(11) Some associations will want to provide a small stipend for their secretary and/or treasurer. If that is desired, substitute the following for Article V Section 7:

"Directors shall not be compensated for their time and effort except that the Secretary (and Treasurer) shall be paid an annual stipend of $____. The Board may authorize officers, directors, and committee members to be paid actual and necessary expenses incurred while on Association business. [Sec. 181.19]"

(12) This section can be dropped if the multiple office holding option is not wanted.

(13) A corporation may choose not to indemnify, in which case the bylaws must explicitly so state. This is not recommended, however.

MISCELLANY

Lunkers for Lunch?

You cast your lure. It plops down between a log and the lily pads and *SPLASH!* The fight is on. Your fishing rod bends. You wrestle the lunker away from snags. It runs. You reel. It jumps! You keep the line taut. It tires. The net comes down and up with a *woosh* and the huge fish is yours. Yours to hang on the wall—yours to fillet and fry—or yours to release.

Release?

Catch and release is a common term today. Not so a few decades ago when fish were considered by most to be a commodity rather than sporting game. Fishing guides rarely suggested their clients release a fish that met the minimum size requirement.

It wasn't until the mid-1970s that conservationists and fishery managers began recommending that angling be regarded as a sport rather than a method of putting food on the table. The idea caught on quickly. Today, more anglers than ever are practicing catch and release on game fish.

There's a problem with taking the largest game fish from a lake. The large fish are usually genetically superior and the best of the breeding stock. Their offspring are likely to become large, healthy adults. When we remove the largest fish and throw back the smaller ones, we are, in a way, guilty of practicing genetic modification. The result could be a lake chockfull of small, stunted fish. The problem doesn't stop there. The smaller of the game fish may not be as effective as predators and populations of panfish or other species might be altered.

The age-old practice of sportsmen keeping the biggest, whether it be largemouth bass, whitetail deer, or any other prey, leaves the smaller, potentially less productive and probably genetically inferior to carry on.

The solution? Let the big ones go. Though it may seem counter to what we learn from childhood on, it is best for the sport, the species, and the lake.

There's another reason to release the biggest of the game fish. Mercury exists in all Wisconsin lakes in varying amounts. The smallest of organisms in the water consume it along with other nutrients. Insects, minnows, and other small predators dine on these organisms. As they do, the mercury slowly builds up in their cells. When other predators, such as panfish, consume the smaller predators, the mercury in their system increases. By the time game fish get large enough to hang on the wall, they have accumulated a far greater amount of mercury than any of the smaller fish. Naturally, the predator at the top of the food chain (aka the angler) gets the most mercury. It's why the DNR issues health warnings about how much fish should be consumed if from a Wisconsin lake or stream. When it comes to mercury, a meal of panfish is far less risky than a meal made from a large bass, northern, or walleye.

Practice *CPR* on Fish: Catch, Photograph, and Release!

- **Many lake fisheries have improved over the past few years because of catch and release programs.**
- **Fighting a fish for an extended time may fatally overexert it. Land it with care, handle it gently, cut the hook if imbedded, and carefully release your catch.**
- **If you measure and photograph your lunker, a taxidermist can make a precise replica for your wall.**
- **Encourage other anglers to practice catch and release, especially with large game fish.**
- **Remember, the fish you release today may be tomorrow's trophy.**

    CPR. It's better for the fish and good for the lake!

The Problem with Catch and Release

This discussion wouldn't be complete without acknowledgement of damage done to the fisheries of some waterbodies by well-meaning anglers *not* keeping enough game fish.

Walleyes and bass compete for the same food and even prey on each other at times. The success of the catch and release philosophy among many anglers has resulted in too many bass being returned to some lakes and streams, altering the balance of species.

Nelson Lake in northwestern Wisconsin was once known as a premier walleye fishery. Sportsmen and their families came from all corners to harvest limits of large walleyed pike. Bass, though present in good numbers, were less likely to be kept. Now, decades after the heyday of walleye fishing on Nelson, the walleye population is very low. Not so the bass, now flourishing not in size but numbers. The resort owners association encourages vacationers to keep all the legal bass they catch. Some resorts will even clean your bass and cook them for you.

The DNR has adjusted the size and bag limits on Nelson Lake and many other waterbodies in order to accommodate fishery populations that have been altered by anglers. In most cases, this means a smaller bag limit and larger size limit on walleyes and northern pike than on bass. Many other lakes and streams now have special regulations for various species in order to best manage our fisheries.

Stand Up for Your Property Rights!

Several decades ago, Wisconsin's legislators recognized the need to protect the value of our individually owned land from poorly planned development. Problems ranged from factories being built in residential areas, to sewage drain fields constructed near a neighbor's well, to many multiple family dwellings constructed too close to each other. It was clear that one person's gain from such development could lead to other people losing property value and the land and water harmed. To help prevent such intrusions on our environment and property values, the State of Wisconsin created a system of model development regulations in 1974. A key component was the use of *zones* appropriate for certain types of development.

With zoning in place, developments on sensitive lands, near sensitive areas, or driven by greed rather than appropriate use of the land became more difficult to initiate. Most counties adopted modified versions of the state plan. Since then, zoning has protected the citizens of Wisconsin from a myriad of poorly planned projects.

The public gains from our zoning regulations. Without regulation, who knows what would be built next door? How might it smell, sound, or affect groundwater? And what might it do to your property value? Zoning rules are meant to protect the property-owning citizen. But they go further.

The history of how we use our land and water goes way back. In 1871, in response to a lawsuit over the transportation of logs across a Wisconsin waterbody, our legislators declared all waters of Wisconsin to be forever free and held in trust for the citizens of Wisconsin. Since then our lakes and streams have been owned not just by the waterfront owners, but by every citizen equally.

Today, we see a significant deterioration of water quality in many of our lakes and streams due to the ever-increasing rise in development. To further protect the value of our properties, including the waterbodies themselves, the state allowed counties to strengthen their zoning rules along the waterfront and in the shoreland zone, thus further protecting the property rights of all

169

Wisconsin citizens who all share ownership of every lake.

Occasionally, those who dislike being told Wisconsin's water resources are more important than their personal gain try to remove control of shoreland zoning regulations from the counties. Should they succeed, they will gain while everyone else loses. We all lose when we venture onto a lake and find the fishery suffering, fewer shore birds, disappearing plants along the shore, unnatural views, and the eyesore of unregulated development. Wisconsin's northern economy also stands to lose if tourists steer clear of our region for cleaner, healthier lakes in neighboring states.

I strongly favor property rights. These include such things as the right from unwanted trespass on private property, the right to buy and sell land, and the right to not have one's property value diminished by the poorly planned developments of others.

If citizens and elected representatives want to protect our properties, including our wonderful lakes and streams, we must be vigilant—always see to it that our shorleland zoning rules are strengthened, not weakened. The lakes belong to you. Stand up for your property rights!

A Case in Point

The following excerpt from an op-ed letter I wrote helps explain the need to recognize the property rights of all citizens, the true owners of Wisconsin's waters.

"The Wisconsin Legislature's deliberate removal of local control of our county's shoreland zoning efforts threatens all surface waters. When the governor approved this in August, 2015, he revoked the promise given to our counties by the state that our county boards are guaranteed to forever have the authority to establish shoreland zoning rules *stronger* than the state's and based on the vulnerability of individual lakes. In the name of property rights, Rep. Adam Jarchow (R – Balsam Lake) and Sen. Tom Tiffany (R – Hazelhurst) removed all counties' ability to establish adequate lake and stream protection.

"In many counties, the minimum frontage requirement for shoreland lots is 150 feet for large lakes, 200 feet for lakes at risk of degradation by overdevelopment, and 300 feet for the most vulnerable lakes. This new legislation threatens to reduce the frontage requirement to 100 feet on all waters. Setbacks and other zoning rules are also affected.

"The Public Trust Doctrine guarantees that our lakes and streams are owned by the public. In Hixon v Public Service, the Supreme Court declared this public right includes the aesthetic qualities of our surface waters and shores. Accordingly, no individual has the right to degrade our waters or diminish the public's enjoyment of them. That's the law. *The right of the public to enjoy clean, safe, healthy waters trumps the right of any individual to use them for personal gain, especially when done at the risk of our water resources.* Creating thousands of 100-foot lots along our shores could devastate our lakes and streams."

Sybil Brakken, photo.

If we are not willing to prepare young people to care for our lakes tomorrow, then why are we working so hard to protect our lakes today?

Operation LEAP: A Lake Education and Appreciation Program for all Wisconsin Students

Operation LEAP is a surface water education activity designed to help Wisconsin youngsters develop good water-related outdoor skills, ethics, boating safety skills, and interest in lakes and streams. LEAP stands for Lake Education and Appreciation Program. It is low in cost, flexible, and user friendly. LEAP can provide a uniform lake education program to all Wisconsin students by the time they finish their public school career. LEAP can do for Wisconsin waters what Driver's Ed has done for our streets and highways.

Operation LEAP will instill good water protection attitudes and habits in our youngsters before bad habits are learned from others. LEAP will save us from having to break bad habits in adults, then re-training them with good attitudes, skills and behaviors—an expensive and time-consuming task. Because of this, LEAP stands to save time and money.

> **LEAP can do for Wisconsin waters what Driver's Ed has done for our streets and highways.**

Operation LEAP's initial target group is fourth grade students. This grade level demonstrates the best readiness, interest, and enthusiasm for the information we present as well as the fast-paced delivery method LEAP provides.

All of our schools introduce Wisconsin history, geography and social studies in grade four. It makes sense to include information on Wisconsin lakes and streams at this age. LEAP would help satisfy Department of Public Instruction requirements in these areas plus meet part of the DPI mandatory science requirement for grade four.

Operation LEAP's second target group is grade seven

174

students. The third target group is grade eleven. Programs will be customized to fit these age groups. Delivery format will change. By the time they leave grade eleven, all students will have been briefly exposed to the proper attitudes, ethics, water safety info, career vignettes, as well as information about lakes, streams, recreational opportunities and more. Ideally, with Operation LEAP, all Wisconsin students will receive information on how and why to protect and preserve lakes.

Although no Wisconsin public school teacher has time to assist with yet another program, LEAP's design actually results in *less* work for the classroom teacher as our pilot program demonstrated. LEAP also meets other DPI requirements giving the classroom teacher additional flexibility. For these reasons, we believe teachers will welcome Operation LEAP into their classrooms.

LEAP can provide a uniform lake education program to all students.

LEAP content can involve many school disciplines including but not limited to art, music, science, literature, history, social studies, computer tech, business skills, and math. Career information, water safety, and basic limnology (study of lakes) are contained within LEAP, as are lake courtesy, ethics, and responsibility.

LEAP uses older students to teach younger students. Both age groups have responded very well to this. High school or middle school science clubs, FFA groups, or conservation clubs can easily administer Operation LEAP. This project uses water education materials already developed and tested. LEAP content is flexible. Local lake associations and conservation clubs can be invited to provide input. This will help address issues important to the lakes in and near the students' community.

Schools choosing Operation LEAP will receive a free "LEAP Kit" containing instructions, materials, and a checklist that helps plan the program. A LEAP CD with many ready-to-print learning activities is also included, along with posters to color, skit materials, templates for carnival games, and other support materials. During the one-week-long Operation LEAP, students will earn tickets for completing simple learning activities related to lakes and lake safety. They will be able to use these tickets to play more learning games during their LEAP Lake Fair.

Operation LEAP week

Because LEAP Week is promoted early, students are eager to participate. They engage in LEAP activities for 1 to 3 hours each day per the following schedule:

- Monday: LAKE GAMES DAY. Students begin earning tickets by successfully completing learning tasks and activities.
- Tuesday: GUEST SPEAKER DAY. A list of suggested speakers is included in the kit.
- Wednesday: TECHNOLOGY DAY. Internet searches of fun, lake related websites.
- Thursday: LEAP LAKE FAIR DAY. Students use their earned tickets to play learsning games and win prizes in a carnival hosted by participating high school students.
- Friday: LEAP GRADUATION. Diploma and treats, pride and recognition.

On Lake Fair Day, the students earn prizes as they learn more about lakes by participating in water-related skits and games that include a secchi disk dip, frog toss, fish feed, fish pond, and other lake contests. At the end of LEAP Week, students receive a diploma and treats. They also take a pledge to help others to be safe and take care of our lakes.

Operation LEAP can be implemented at no cost to the school, other than minor printing (less than 25¢ per student). LEAP can be funded by contributions from local lake associations, sporting clubs, community clubs, business firms, or school fundraisers. Cost per student varies by community and local needs. Carnival prizes can be ordered for approximately $1 per student. Prizes such as pencils, stickers and posters are available from the US Forest Service, DNR, local businesses, and community organizations. Diplomas, word puzzles, and

worksheets can be printed by the school. Carnival games are easily made by high school volunteers using basic materials and simple LEAP kit instructions.

Operation LEAP satisfies a component of the Wisconsin Lakes Partnership strategic plan. The Wisconsin Association of Lakes resolved to continue development of LEAP as a means to protect our lakes by educating our citizens at an early age. The DNR has approved a Lakes Planning Grant to pursue further development of LEAP. Other funding is likely as LEAP progresses.

Operation LEAP is likely to receive great community support because of its enormous potential to protect our lakes. Many lake associations, sporting clubs, community clubs, towns, cities, and chambers of commerce are likely to welcome and support LEAP.

LEAP offers children the opportunity to become involved in positive activities aimed at helping our environment. Local government and business leaders are likely to show support. Parents admire the program as do school administrators, teachers, and local lake association members.

Most important, LEAP is a hit with the kids because it is fun, rewarding, and gives them a sense of accomplishment.

The following pages contain some of the content of Operation LEAP.

Your School's OPERATION LEAP Schedule and Checklist
(Modify to fit your needs.)

Operation LEAP is a special program designed to help youngsters learn how they can safely enjoy our lakes and protect them at the same time. **Operation LEAP (for Lake Education and Appreciation Project) will be a full week of lake education activities, water safety training, and related lake protection information for youngsters.** With help from high school student volunteers we call "lake leaders," LEAP will offer 4th graders the tools they need to understand why our lakes need their care and how they can safely enjoy and benefit from our lakes without causing the lakes nor themselves any harm. They will also gain a sense of pride, ownership, and reward as they learn that they can protect their lakes.

Monday   Introduction and **LAKE GAMES DAY.** Emphasis on boating safety, responsible lake use and lake protection. Student lake leaders will visit the classroom to explain the reason for LEAP week and how the youngsters can earn rewards by participating. Next, they'll pass out

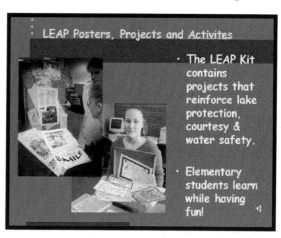

worksheets, puzzles, printed games, and coloring sheets, provided in the kit. Students will earn tickets for the lake fair activities by completing these learning tasks. Also, class divides into five groups for skit practice. Assign skits (from poster series provided.) One *Lake Leader* assigned to each group. Be sure to take photos of the activities.

178

Tuesday   **SPECIAL GUEST DAY.** (Potential media event.) Guest speaker will offer information. Emphasis on water safety, limnology, or aquatic biology. Brief mention of careers and the rewards of working with lakes. In the Q & A time after speech, tickets will be offered to students with questions. Following the presentation(s), questions may be asked by the high school lake leaders about information presented by speakers. Tickets to those with the correct answer. Certificate of appreciation given to the speaker. Take photos &/or videotape.

Wednesday   **TECHNOLOGY DAY.** (Potential media event.) Everyone meets in the computer lab where high school leader and helpers host a tour of the internet with emphasis on websites focused on lake protection. Scavenger hunt format. Students will earn tickets based on those web items they discover during the session. Take photographs.

Thursday   **LAKE FAIR DAY.** (Definite media event.) High school lake leaders set up booths, contests, games, etc., at a special location. (In our case, the old gymnasium.) Everyone meets at the lake fair where we spend our tickets at the fishpond, lily pad toss, frog jump, secchi disk dip, and other games. Also have some relay races, contests, and skits. Any students who did not earn enough tickets in previous days can go to the ticket booth where they can get a ticket for answering a random lake question correctly. Everyone helps clean up the area at end of Lake Fair in a contest reflective of a litter clean-up. Photograph and/or videotape.

Friday   **Operation LEAP AWARDS DAY.** (Potential media event.) In this final meeting, a high school lake leader will remind the students of the need to protect our lakes and to be safe when near the water, plus the benefits of being a conservationist. LEAP Graduation Diplomas are then given to each student along with any leftover prizes. Guests, such as local lake association members, school or community officials, parents, can attend. Treats are provided. Take photos.

Operation LEAP Checklist

Prior to LEAP Week:

☐ Invite 5 to 10 interested high school *Lake Leader*s to participate. Assign one *Lake Leader* as the LEAP Photographer. This student will post pictures on the school website or social media every day and get some photos of the planning and preparation. Assign a student leader to each day. All others will assist as needed.

☐ Create a file and save everything for future reference.

☐ Prepare a draft schedule for the 5-day event. (See page 1) Include lake courtesy, lake protection, fish and other critters both in and near the lake, aquatic plants, pollution, water/boating safety, rewards of stewardship and careers. Use materials provided with Operation LEAP kit.

☐ Contact local businesses for contribution of prizes, treats, funds if necessary. Purchase prizes if possible and needed. (Inexpensive prizes can come from the Dollar Store, Omaha Trading Co.)

☐ Ask a local lake association to partner by providing a volunteer to present Friday's diplomas. (Our school principal did this.) Other volunteers could help with lake fair day. Lake association could provide some treats or prizes.

☐ Contact the teacher (s) of the target group for permission and to arrange the event to fit teacher's schedule. (In our case, grade 4 in our elementary school.)

☐ Reserve room (s) for mini-lake fair, computer activities, other activities, as needed.

☐ Inform building supervisor (s) and head custodian of the event.

☐ Invite other teachers to participate with the planning.

☐ Contact DNR, local lake association, others, for speakers. Consider fisheries manager, game warden, limnologist.

☐ Contact DNR, UWEX, WL and others for some of the materials, handouts, etc.

☐ Meet as needed with *Lake Leader*s to finalize schedule and prepare for the week.

- ☐ Contact media to have coverage for at least one of the daily activities.
- ☐ Send a note home to parents informing them of their student's participation in the event. Invite them to attend one of the functions.
- ☐ Organize all handouts, materials, games, prizes, etc.
- ☐ Create posters publicizing the event. Younger students can help to generate their interest in the event. Post in school and community.
- ☐ Print certificates of appreciation for speakers, volunteers, and prize donors. Print LEAP graduation diplomas with names of the students.
- ☐ Take photos of high school student lake leaders preparing for the event. (Making posters, planning meetings, etc.)
- ☐ Call to confirm speakers and media.
- ☐ Meet with lake leaders to make final preparations.

Follow up:
- ☐ Send thank you letters to speakers, volunteers, supporting firms, and agencies.
- ☐ Create a photo display and a display of supporting firms and organizations.
- ☐ Get classroom teacher and student feedback on how to improve next year's event.
- ☐ Submit a post-LEAP press release to local newspaper, Wisconsin Lakes and UWEX – Lakes for their newsletters and other publications.
- ☐ Get a write-up in school newsletter, yearbook, local lake association newsletter. Include a list of supporting firms and organizations.
- ☐ Throw a pizza party for the Lake Leaders and appropriate volunteers. Local lake organization may want this assignment.

A Brief Report on *Operation LEAP*, a Lake Education and Appreciation Program for Elementary Students in Wisconsin's Public Schools

The pilot project for Operation LEAP was held at the New Auburn School during the final week of February, 2002. The event was regarded as highly successful by the participating elementary students, our assisting high school students, teachers, administrators, and parents.

The event began with planning and fundraising in January. Our high school student "lake leaders" found ample boating safety and lake education information available online from a wide variety of sources. The lake leaders chose the materials, activities and games for the week.

The 4th grade was eager to begin on Monday. Most students completed all of the activities offered, indicating a need for additional activities and projects. The students worked hard to complete the various learning activities, knowing that each completion would result in a ticket for the upcoming LEAP Lake Fair games. Tuesday's guest speaker enjoyed an attentive 4th grade audience with many good questions. Wednesday's Technology Day was equally successful. All students found the recommended websites they were assigned. All received tickets as rewards.

Thursday's LEAP Lake Fair carnival went very well. We learned that we should have practiced our lake skits earlier, rather than making them up on the spot. We had planned on running some relay races, such as leap frog and duck walk to fill extra time. But because the students were well occupied by the learning games and activities, we had no time for the relay races. The Lake Fair lasted 90 minutes. Activities included the secchi disk dip, where students checked the clarity of colored water in a large trash container, Frog Feed, a bean bag toss, a fish pond, Frog Jump, and a fishing board game created by one of our high

182

school student lake leaders. Children who ran short of tickets earned more by answering lake questions at the ticket booth. Everyone left with many prizes and more knowledge about lakes and lake safety.

Friday's LEAP graduation also ran smoothly. The students were proud to receive their diplomas. They took a pledge to help others be safe and take care of our lakes. They were given the remaining prizes and a few minutes to investigate them.

The Operation LEAP pilot was a success with plenty of opportunities to revise, refine and redesign. The students learned about lakes and lake safety. They had fun while they learned. The classroom teacher was not burdened and, in fact, gained extra planning time because of our LEAP activities. This is important if we hope to get the classroom teachers to welcome

LEAP. The high school students enjoyed the week and the rewards of being able to help the younger students and the post LEAP reflection activities. It is likely Operation LEAP would be welcomed in other schools. LEAP could have a long term positive effect on those who engage in the program. This effect could be not unlike the effect Drivers' Education has had on motorists. If we imagine what our highways and streets might be like without Drivers' Ed, we may begin to see the potential of this intense, focused lake education and appreciation program. LEAP's end result could benefit our lakes, lake organizations, communities, enforcement, and all those who work to protect our lakes while providing for greater safety for our students while on the water.

Dinosaurs, Ice, and a Hole in the Roof

As I write, the frozen lake beyond the window is rumbling thunderously from four days of sub-zero temperatures. It's almost as though the lake is announcing its displeasure with the acute cold. The deep rolling bellows are caused by expansion and cracking of the thirty-inch-thick ice and will continue into late March or early April when longer days and warm sunshine will quiet the lake again.

In my youth, I imagined these rumblings to be the calls of the great dinosaurs that inhabited this land eons before the glaciers shaped the landscape we now know. I recently learned from a University of Wisconsin geologist that our lake was most likely created by several enormous pieces of glacial ice. Some ten thousand years ago, the mile-high glacier slowly receded as the climate warmed. Melting and erosion at ground level caused huge ice caves. Top-heavy, frozen projections of ice, some weighing thousands upon thousands of tons, would break free and fall, embedding deep into the earth. Long after the glacier receded, the ice remained, protected by the insulating soil surrounding it. In time, the sun prevailed and temperatures moderated, leaving deep, water-filled pockets in the ground. These eventually became the "holes" found in many of our northern lakes, including the one beyond my windows.

Not long ago I attended a meeting of waterfront owners at a neighboring lake. They met to explore the idea of forming a lake association. Like most initial, exploratory meetings, those attending brought good comments, questions, and a few concerns. Some of the concerns centered on why such an organization is needed at all. Such skepticism is often a typical response when a lake association is proposed.

In spite of the fact that some Wisconsin lakes have had successful associations for over a century, some people fail to see the need for such citizen-run lake management groups. Things have gone all right thus far, so why establish another organization that might make decisions affecting others on the lake? They ask why organize at all until a problem surfaces?

184

I recall a story of a fellow who had a hole in his roof. On clear days, he saw no reason to fix that hole. After all, it wasn't raining. On rainy days, the water poured in through that hole. But what could he do? Climbing up on the roof in the rain was now both difficult and dangerous. So he waited for clear weather when, of course, the work again went undone.

Perhaps folks working to organize on that neighboring lake won't see the real benefit of a lake association until they experience one of those rainy days. Sure, we can all hope for sunshine, but shouldn't we prepare for foul weather, too? That "foul weather" might come in the form of a new invasive species being established in the lake. Or bulldozers clearing the waterfront for a resort, tavern, or campground. Perhaps a marina or a condominium or a pipeline or a power line. With a lake association in place, those folks can work together in response to whatever issue comes along. Folks working together can speak with a united voice and influence the direction and attitude of the surrounding community toward use and care of the lake. Even those waterfront owners who choose to not actively participate in the lake association should understand the benefit of having others watching out for lake issues that might arise. Even if they choose to remain inactive, they should join, if only to amplify the volume of the association's united voice when needed.

Some say the Department of Natural Resources will take care of the lake. Though it's true the DNR employs many skilled scientists and other workers to monitor our lakes, their work stops at the water's edge. It is our county boards who make the rules about what happens on shore. But county rules affecting use of the shorelands often lack the strength to protect the water. Also, there is the inability of county zoning officials to adequately enforce the rules due to staffing shortages. Even when they are able to inspect, strict laws prohibit zoning officials from entering private property without permission. Add to this the fact that both county officials and DNR employees are prohibited by law from lobbying for better laws and more funding to increase staffing needed to resolve the above issues.

On the other hand, a lake association is an independent group of citizens with the legal right to influence local, county, state, and even the federal government for the benefit of the community—influence them for the good of the lake. Lake associations are usually comprised of like-minded people speaking with one united voice—people working to affect positive change.

The next time you find yourself gazing across the lake, imagine enormous ice chunks breaking free from the mother glacier and falling most of a mile before driving deep into the earth before you. Imagine then the changes this land must have experienced during the thousands of years between that ice and the arrival of the European settlers. How beautiful our lakes must have looked to the Native Americans, explorers, the fur traders, and timber cruisers who canoed here.

We can only imagine how our lakes looked to these original visitors over a century ago. But we can do more than imagine how they will look a century from now. Working together, speaking with one united voice, we have the opportunity to protect our lakes and provide clean, safe, healthy waters for ourselves and for all future generations.

Seaplanes and the New Boating Laws

Wisconsin's recent law prohibiting transport of aquatic plants and animals now addresses an issue that previously received little attention: seaplanes. Because these specialized aircraft are able to land on water, they pose a special challenge to our lakes and their respective lake associations.

The floats of seaplanes can carry invasive plants and animals from one lake to another without being noticed by our Clean Boats, Clean Waters landing monitors or game wardens. The Bayfield County Lakes Forum (BCLF) conducted a survey of many lake association members. Based on the results, the Forum came to several conclusions including this: *due to the inability of the pilot to inspect the floats, there must be no landings or takeoffs from lakes known to be infested with aquatic invasive species (AIS).* Today, in light of the new law prohibiting transport of invasive plants and animals, seaplanes must be treated as any other watercraft.

In a letter to the county board, BCLF asked that no plane be allowed to land on any Bayfield County waters if it came from any waterbody in or out of the county that has Eurasian water milfoil, Zebra Mussels, curly leaf pondweed or any other form of aquatic invasive species as identified on the WDNR AIS list. The Forum directors offered the county the following recommendations:

- Any lake or river that contains any species on the WDNR AIS list *must* be ordered off limits to seaplanes due to the inability of the pilot to clean the floats between taking off and landing.
- Planes coming from any waterbody known to be infested with any aquatic invasive species, within or beyond Bayfield County, must be specifically prohibited from landing on *all* Bayfield County waterbodies, including any portion of Lake Superior that falls within county jurisdiction.

Our consideration of the lake association seaplane survey also led to the following statements:

- The Bayfield County Lakes Forum is not opposed to the use of seaplanes on waterbodies that are large enough to accommodate them in a safe, reasonable, and responsible fashion.
- All slow-no-wake laws required of boaters including the new 100-foot-from-shore rule must be followed to the letter by seaplane pilots.
- For safety purposes, our DNR game wardens and lake associations should be advised which lakes will be used by seaplanes and when this will occur.
- Pilots should be encouraged to practice touch and go landings and take-offs *only* on very large bodies of water and never on small lakes.
- Lakes within thirty minutes of an airport should be off limits to seaplanes as there is no real need to fly to a lake when an airport is close.
- All fuel spills must be immediately reported to the Sheriff and immediately cleaned up. This rule should be enforced with a substantial penalty due to the potential damage to a waterbody and expense to our local governments.
- Lake associations should be consulted before any county board decision is made regarding the use of seaplanes on the waters served by those associations.
- The County must post a list of those lakes that are acceptable for float plane use.

The BCLF does not discourage any form of transportation or recreation as long as the laws and precautions others must follow are not disregarded. We all have a responsibility to protect the natural resources we enjoy. The Forum applauds those pilots and all others who rank the preservation of our pristine waters higher than their own personal pleasure.

Guard Against Melanoma when on the Water

The Northwest Wisconsin Waters Consortium (Northwest Waters) is working to increase awareness of the risk of melanoma. Because our time enjoying Wisconsin's lakes often has people out in the sun for long periods of time, and because the reflective quality of the water magnifies the amount of ultraviolet (UV) light exposure we receive, it is very important that we protect ourselves and our children against this potentially fatal health threat. Waldo Asp is the past-president of Northwest Waters, a consortium of countywide lake management and conservation groups. He recommends that, before going out on the water, we consider these important health facts:

1. There are over one million new cases of skin cancer diagnosed in the U.S. each year, outnumbering the total number of all other cancers combined.
2. Over ten thousand Americans die each year from melanoma. This is more than one person every hour.
3. Annually, the costs of treating this type of skin cancer are over one billion dollars. However, the emotional and physical costs are incalculable.
4. Less than one third of our children are protected from too much sun exposure at home, school, and at the lake.
5. In addition to sun exposure, use of tanning salons increases the risk of melanoma. This may account for a greater rise in melanoma cases among young women than in men.
6. Doctors rarely find melanomas. The patient usually does. Therefore, practice self-examination regularly.
7. Those born this year have a 1 in 50 chance of getting melanoma.
8. Due to late detection, men have a higher death rate for melanoma than do women.
9. Melanoma is the easiest cancer to screen and detect early, but it is also the least screened-for type of cancer.

Northwest Waters urges everyone to:

- Avoid direct exposure to the sun during midday hours.
- Always use a high-SPF sunscreen and lip balm.
- Reapply sunscreen every two hours and more often when sweating or swimming.
- When in direct sunlight, wear a wide-brimmed hat, tightly woven clothing, and sunglasses.
- Protect your children. Set a good example for them.
- When possible, seek shade when outdoors.
- Remember that the shorter the shadow you cast, the greater your risk from UV exposure.
- Avoid tanning parlors and sunlamps.

"It is especially important to teach youngsters that mid-summer sunlight needs to be enjoyed in moderation," said Asp. "Limiting our exposure to direct sunlight during the middle of the day and using sunscreen are just common sense. Northwest Waters hopes that all your time spent on the water is relaxing, rewarding, and safe. Enjoy our northwest Wisconsin lakes and streams, but do it safely."

Resources to Support Sustainable Lakes, Streams, and Shorelands

(Quick links to the online resources below are on the *Saving Our Lakes & Streams* web page at BadgerValley.com. Scan the QR code above, then visit the BVP web page where you can pull up any of the following resources.)

Wisconsin Lakes (WL)

- **WL's Website:** Provides many resources for lake groups and individuals, as well as information about WL's educational events, accomplishments, publications, and the benefits of becoming a member. *www.wisconsinlakes.org*
- **E-Lake Letter**: WL's e-mail news bulletin keeps lake enthusiasts informed of topics that affect all Wisconsin lakes. (Free service.) *wisconsinlakes.org/index.php/elake-letter.*
- **Lake Connection**: Wisconsin Lakes' quarterly periodical, available in both print and electronic form. Explores lake issues and offers compelling and inspiring stories of lake organizations and citizens doing good things for lakes. All lake association members are entitled to free electronic delivery. See *http://wisconsinlakes.org.*

UW Extension – Lakes Program

- **UWEX - Lakes website** provides resources on starting and effectively managing lake organizations. It includes the "Lake List," a searchable online directory of Wisconsin lake organizations and lake-related businesses servicing them. The website also offers a history of the Wisconsin Lakes Partnership and *The Water Way*, a statewide strategic plan for our lakes. *www.uwsp.edu/cnr/uwexlakes* (Free service.)
- **Lake Tides: The UW-Extension Lakes Program newsletter.** A superb quarterly newsletter addressing a wide variety of issues affecting Wisconsin's lakes and streams. (Free service.) Sign up to receive your copy or view archived editions at: *www.uwsp.edu/dnr/uwexlakes/laketides* or *http://bit.ly/1kKmKQP*

- *People of the Lakes: A Guide for Wisconsin Lake Organizations.* Good reference book for lake associations and districts. UW Extension publication G3818

From the WI DNR Lakes Program:
- **Wisconsin DNR Lakes Program website:** Provides lakes and rivers grants guidelines, applications, example reports and plans; lake management tools; lake maps; citizen-based lake monitoring resources; boating, fishing, and hunting regulations; a statewide directory of DNR staff, and more. Find it at *www.dnr.wi.gov/org/water/fhp/lakes*
- **Environmental Education for Kids (EEK!)** An online educational conservation magazine for kids. Offers a wide variety of activities and fun learning opportunities. *dnr.wi.gov/eek*
- **Into the Outdoors:** A weekly television program for children of all ages. Science education that empowers individuals and classrooms to think critically about Planet Earth. Also available online at *intotheoutdoors.org.*
- **Wisconsin Conservation Congress:** Offers opportunities to post resolutions supporting good conservation regulations in Wisconsin at the annual Spring Hearings, held in April. See *dnr.wi.gov/about/wcc/* for more information.

From the Bayfield County Lakes Forum (BCLF):
- **BCLF website:** Provides information directly related to the health of northern Wisconsin lakes, streams, and watersheds. Website includes many lake-related newsletter articles and photos that are free for non-profit use in lake organization newsletters. *BayfieldCountyLakes.org.*

How to find your U.S. Legislators:
- *www.opencongress.org/people/zipcodelookup*

How to find your Wisconsin Legislators:
- *maps.legis.wisconsin.gov/*

Lead Toxicity in Lakes and Streams:

- **LoonWatch:** Maintains a list of non-lead tackle suppliers. *northland.edu/loonwatch*
- **Raptor Education Group:** *raptoreducationgroup.org*
- **DNR on lead:** *dnr.wi.gov/fish/pages/gettheleadout.html*

Other resources:

- **Dan Small Outdoors Radio** On-demand streaming of current show & archives. Listen to a variety of Dan's award-winning Wisconsin outdoor radio shows. *dansmalloutdoors.com/*
- **Outdoor Wisconsin:** Milwaukee Public TV's award-winning outdoor show. Takes viewers to all parts of the state in all four seasons. Includes hunting, fishing, camping, biking, conservation, wildlife observation, and outdoor safety. Archives and station information at *mptv.org/localshows/outdoor_wisconsin*
- **Wisconsin Academy of Sciences, Arts & Letters:** Inland Lakes *http://www.wisconsinacademy.org/tags/inland-lakes*
- **"Communicating About Water: A Wisconsin Toolkit"** An excellent paper by the Wisconsin Academy to help citizen volunteers speak clearly about water issues. *http://www.wisconsinacademy.org/sites/default/files/WOW_CommunicationsKit_2014%20-%20Copy.pdf*
- **Countywide Lake Associations:** Most of the 26 countywide lake associations offer websites containing information pertaining to regional issues. Find the entire list at *wisconsinlakes.org/index.php/countywide-lake-associations*
- **The North American Lake Management Society (NALMS):** Members include statewide lake associations, business partners, educators and members of the science community. *nalms.org*
- **Wisconsin League of Conservation Voters:** Advocates good conservation. Keeps close track of votes on conservation legislation. You can track your legislator's attitude toward the environment at *conservationvoters.org.*
- *Lakescaping for Wildlife & Water Quality* available at *www.minnesotasbookstore.com.*

193

- **Wisconsin Wetlands Association:** Protecting the state's wetland resources through education, training, advocacy, and research on key wetlands issues. *WisconsinWetlands.org*
- **Wisconsin Wildlife Federation:** Protects fish & wildlife habitat (clean air & water, healthy forests & grasslands) via conservation education & advocacy of sound state & federal policies. *wiwf.org*
- **Rivers Alliance of Wisconsin:** Strong advocates for protection, enhancement, & restoration of rivers and watersheds. Search for news about your favorite river. *www.wisconsinrivers.org*
- **Wisconsin Land Trust Alliance:** Search by county and state through a comprehensive list of land trust organizations *findalandtrust.org/states/wisconsin55*
- **Gathering Waters Conservancy:** Assists land trusts, landowners and communities in their efforts to protect the state's land and water resources. *GatheringWaters.org*
- **Wisconsin Water Library.** A variety of information, including assorted pages for adults and youngsters. *https://aqua.wisc.edu/Waterlibrary*

<u>Websites for kids:</u> The following websites offer water-related conservation activities for youngsters:
- *water.epa.gov/learn/kids*
- *cwf-fcf.org/en/discover-wildlife/for-kids*
- *ga.water.usgs.gov/edu*
- *nefsc.noaa.gov/faq/index.html*
- *usefultrivia.com/science_trivia/fish_trivia_index.html*
- *https://aqua.wisc.edu/Waterlibrary*

(Quick links to these online resources are on the *Saving Our Lakes & Streams* web page at BadgerValley.com. Scan the QR code, then visit the BVP web page where you can pull up most of the above resources and information about other Badger Valley Publishing books.)

The Treasure of Namakagon
James Brakken's "flagship" lumberjack novel.
Book 1 in the award-winning Chief Namakagon trilogy:

2nd PLACE WINNER out of 10,000 worldwide entries in the 2013 *Amazon Breakthrough Novel Award* competition!

A young lumberjack, his Indian mentor, and a lost silver mine—a fact-based tale of timber, treasure, and treachery in America's 19th century wilderness. Following a daring rescue from a dangerous child-labor scheme in 1883 Chicago, an orphan is plunged into the peak of lumberjack life in far northwestern Wisconsin. There, an Ojibwe chief teaches him respect for nature and shows him to hidden treasure—an actual mine, lost when the chief died in 1886 and yet to be rediscovered.

You'll meet young Tor Loken whose family owns a wilderness lumber camp. You'll join the fight when a sinister timber tycoon takes control of the river, threatening the Loken's future and the lumberjacks' dollar-a-day pay. You'll be in the cook shanty before dawn for breakfast, then out into the cuttings where, knee deep in snow, you'll help harvest giant pine logs. Hitch the Clydesdales to the tanker. Ice the trails for the giant timber sleighs. Take the train to town but keep one eye peeled for hooligans seeking an easy swindle.

Back in the bunkhouse, spin a yarn with colorful lumberjack friends. Next, it's a Saturday night of merriment in town. Dress warmly, though. It's a three hour sleigh ride back to camp at twenty below zero.

Come spring, you'll drive the timber down a thundering, icy river, jumping log to log as they rush downstream, danger around each bend. Finally, payday! Time to celebrate. Keep your pocketbook buttoned up, though. Scoundrels are eager to separate you from your winter wages.

Put on your red wool mackinaw. Grab your pike pole. You are about to plunge into 19th century lumberjack life *The Treasure of Namakagon*, a thrilling adventure, thick with twists and turns, researched and illustrated by an author who lives there.

And, yes, the boy wins the girl's heart.

Also at BadgerValley.com: Book 2 in the Chief Namakagon trilogy:

Tor Loken and the Death of Chief Namakagon

Lace your calked boots and button your mackinaw once again. You are about to plunge into a twisting, turning, thrilling north woods mystery: *Tor Loken and the Death of Chief Namakagon.*

Based on the suspicious death of Chief Namakagon in 1886, this tale depicts a time when rugged lumberjacks and miners brought civilization and wealth to Wisconsin's wilderness, while corrupt, ruthless opportunists devoured all they could.

Following a devastating blizzard, Namakagon's body is discovered near a secluded silver mine. Only nineteen-year-old Tor Loken can prove murder. Suspicious accidents soon plague his father's lumber camp. Tor and his sweetheart, Rosie, risk their lives to capture the killer and protect the tribal treasure. With you, they will solve the dark mystery surrounding Namakagon's murder in this fast-paced, fact-based thriller by the award-winning Wisconsin author whose research now unlocks the truth.

History tells us Chief Namakagon traded silver for supplies in Ashland in the 1880s. Several miners tried to get him to disclose the source of his silver. One man came close but, when a large bear blocked their trail, Namakagon took this for a bad omen and refused to continue. Following a fierce 1886 blizzard, Namakagon's remains were found along a trail that may have been very near his silver cache. Many suspect he met with foul play. Suspicions remain regarding the cause of his death. The location of the lost silver is still unknown.

In this mystery-adventure, Tor loses his mentor during this snowstorm. Tor is determined to solve the mystery of Namakagon's death. Suspicious accidents plague the Loken camp as Tor and Rosie risk all to stop the murderer.

Learn more about the rich history of the lumberjack days, help solve the mystery, and gather your own clues about the likely location of the legendary silver mine of Chief Namakagon.

243 pages. Illustrated. Written for adults though suitable for age twelve and up. **Maps to the 19th century Marengo silver fields, the likely location of Chief Namakagon's lost silver mine, are included in this novel.** This is a thrilling read and a book you will treasure in more ways than one! Available at select outlets and BadgerValley.com.

Grab a paddle and step into your birch bark canoe. You're off to the early 1800s and a fascinating, factual dramatization of the early life of Old Ice Feathers. It is a novel you won't be able to put down.

Book 3 in the trilogy:
The Secret Life of Chief Namakagon

When his friend and mentor dies in 1886, young Tor Loken learns of Namakagon's previous life. But why, four decades earlier, did he isolate himself in this uninhabited northern Wisconsin wilderness? Was Namakagon running from a troubled past?

Now James Brakken's research reveals Namakagon's life *before** he came to his northern Wisconsin home. His is an amazing true-life adventure—a tale of a child abduction by renegades, then 30 years living as an Ojibwe. Caught in the middle of a bloody war between the Hudson's Bay Company and the North West Fur Company, his people reject him. He tries living among the Whites but is unable to adjust. Loved by few and despised by many, he can't find his niche in life—a life torn in two by others. All odds are against him until he meets a doctor who helps him write a book about his life with the Indians. But even his highly successful book cannot stop his downward spiral.

Then, accused of murder in 1846, he flees and begins a new life, that of an Indian hermit in northwest Wisconsin where he becomes Ice Feathers and discovers a secret silver mine. (A map in this book gives the best clue yet to the lost mine's likely whereabouts.)

These adventure-filled pages unveil Chief Namakagon's secret and offer a captivating, stand-alone novel written for all readers who enjoy a fusion of thrilling fiction and fascinating history. This illustrated novel is suitable for readers age twelve and up.

*Since northern Wisconsin was settled in the 1880s, nobody knew that Chief Namakagon was actually a man who disappeared after being accused of a Michigan murder in 1846. When, in 2014, James Brakken's research verified the "original" identity of Chief Namakagon, he solved a 168-year-old cold case that historians have pondered for more than a century.

Find your *TREASURE* and other James Brakken books only at select Indy bookstores, historical museums, and preferred outlets. Free sample excerpts, discounts and secure online credit card ordering is available at James Brakken's official website, BadgerValley.com. Written for young and old. *Made in USA.*

The Early Life and True Identity of Chief Namakagon
If it waddles like a duck and quacks like a duck ...

When, in 2008, I began *The Treasure of Namakagon,* I did not intend to write a sequel, much less a trilogy. But research for book one led me to these two conclusions: 1, the chief really did refuse to disclose where he was getting silver. And, 2, his death involved foul play. Compelled to share what I discovered about his silver mine and the suspicious facts surrounding his death. I wrote *The Death of Chief Namakagon,* a fact-filled murder mystery.

My research soon had me wondering why, in the mid-1840s, this man came to a remote, uninhabited lake in northern Wisconsin to live a hermit's life. Why did he isolate himself in this distant place? And how was it he could speak English, extraordinarily uncommon of natives then?

I imagine the November, 1880 arrival of the railway turned his life on end, especially when newspaperman, George Thomas, stepped off the train and sought out the only English-speaking, long-time resident of the area. The reporter's interview helped answer some of my questions: According to Thomas, Namakagon came from Sault Ste. Marie decades earlier. Why? Because a dream revealed a fire and a death. Thomas wrote that this dream made Namakagon fear he'd be executed for a murder he did not commit.

By itself, this statement shed no light on my search for his previous life. So I traveled to the Sault where a deeper investigation revealed a murder *had* occurred there—in 1846. Fearing execution, the accused man fled—*a statement nearly identical to that given by Namakagon to George Thomas!*

I exposed many more clues and convincing details, but positive proof came while scouring the old land records, looking for the location of his silver mine. *The official records, buried for decades, disclosed the "early" identity of Chief Namakagon.* Eureka! I'd solved a *168-year-old cold case*—the solution to the 1846 disappearance of an innocent man wanted for a cold-blooded murder. The official government land records, along with the sheer number of clues, statements, and facts provided by professional historians, were clear evidence that the hermit of Lake Namakagon was, indeed, a fugitive who hid for forty years in the Wisconsin wilderness. I'd unveiled compelling, reliable verification of Namakagon's early life.

So, research for my fact-based murder mystery, *The Death of Chief Namakagon,* led me to write *The Secret Life of Chief Namakagon,* a book about the first half of his life. It's a fascinating, wilderness adventure based on his own words and those of historians—historians who, by the way, knew only part of his colorful life. My first two Chief Namakagon books shed light on the final half of his intriguing life and still-suspicious death.

Secret is a window into the world of a woodsman with an amazing history, an adventurer, a war hero who evaded death many times, a celebrated author forced to turn fugitive and become Mikwam-mi-Miguan, or Ice Feathers, the legendary hermit we now call Chief Namakagon.

Take pleasure in sharing his journey and learning his story in book three of the trilogy, *The Secret Life of Chief Namakagon.*

DARK - A CAMPFIRE COMPANION
by James A. Brakken

56 very scary short stories & delightfully frightening poems. Spine-tingling tales of ghosts, dragons, ne'er-do-wells, and monsters—each waiting to raise goosebumps. Every story is morbidly illustrated by long-dead master artists of the mac abre. Chilling, yet wonderful fireside reading. A "must-have" for every cabin bookshelf and home library. Ages 12 and up.

THE MOOSE & WILBUR P. DILBY
Plus 36 Fairly True Tales from Up North.
by James A. Brakken

Thirty-seven short stories straight from the heart & the heart of the north. All fairly true, more or less. Some are sad, some shocking, most are hilarious. Small town tales of baseball, fishing, and hunting, tavern tales, jokesters, murderers, gangsters, and flimflam men. Lost treasure, lumberjacks, and legends of the north. Includes a 1-act play and several short stories based on the Chief Namakagon trilogy. Written for adults but fine for age 12. **Features *two* 1ˢᵗ place award-winning stories.**

DISCOVERING AMERICA
ONE MARATHON AT A TIME
by Jim Anderson

Told he was too old to run a marathon in every state, Jim Anderson laced up his running shoes and, at the age of 51, took the challenge. Twelve years later, he completed his goal, gaining a unique appreciation for our nation and its history. It's a tour of America as experienced through the eyes and words of a runner on a quest to compete in a marathon in every state. Illustrated. All ages.

Coming soon: A thrilling, often harrowing, true tale of an amazing Wisconsin Indian agent in the mid-1800s whose actions affect today's life and culture.
Watch for **THE BENJAMIN ARMSTRONG STORY** *in 2016.*

Secure online ordering or download an order form at <u>BadgerValley.com</u> where shipping is free!

BADGER VALLEY PUBLISHING
45255 East Cable Lake Road
Cable, Wisconsin 54821   715-798-3163
Email TreasureofNamakagon@Gmail.com
Badger Valley can publish YOUR book, too!
Now accepting new book proposals.

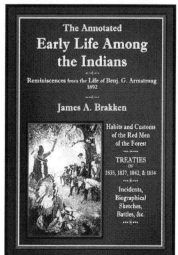

About the Author

James Brakken lives in northern Wisconsin's water-rich Bayfield County within an afternoon's drive of thousands of lakes and many miles of streams.

In 1994, concerned about reports of problems affecting many Wisconsin lakes, he and his wife, Sybil, organized a community discussion of issues that might affect the lake where he owned a cabin. That conversation led to the origin of the Cable Lakes Association, a conservation organization active in lake protection since its founding. In 1995, James established an environmental club at the school where he taught. The club focused on sharing knowledge about lake protection issues. His New Auburn High School *Lakes Project* students went on to become the only student conservation club to win the coveted Wisconsin Lake Stewardship Award twice.

In September 2000, Brakken took his *Lakes Project* student leaders to Washington where they met with legislators and EPA officials. There, on behalf of all youngsters who swim, fish, and play in America's lakes, his students lobbied for funding of EPA's Clean Waters Act. Other lobbyists included Trout Unlimited, the Isaac Walton League, and the North American Lakes Management Society. President Bill Clinton later approved $250 million for the EPA Clean Waters program. The following year, Brakken became the 2001 recipient of his own Wisconsin Lakes Stewardship Award in the Individual category.

In addition to laying the foundation for the Cable Lakes Association, Brakken co-founded the Bayfield County Lakes Forum and the Northwest Wisconsin Waters Consortium, presiding, at times, over all three.

In 1998, while serving on the Board of Directors of the Wisconsin Association of Lakes, Brakken proposed a boating safety law intended to protect boaters and swimmers as well as the near-shore areas of all Wisconsin waters. After a twelve-year, roller coaster effort, his 100-foot-from-shore slow-no-wake proposal became state law, protecting the plants and animals that depend on these waters as well as all who play there.

The author's two decades of experience working with local, countywide, and statewide lake and river management organizations is reflected within these pages. This collection and James Brakken's simple suggestions on how to help protect our waters are offered to all who cherish clean, safe, healthy lakes and streams for today and tomorrow.

Awards and Honors:
Wisconsin Lakes Director Emeritus & Past President
Northwest Waters Consortium President
Bayfield County Lakes Forum Past President
Cable Lakes Association Past President
Namekagon River Partnership Director
2001 Wisconsin Lakes Stewardship Award
2013, 2014, & 2016 Lake Superior Writers Award
2014 Wisconsin Writers Association *Jade Ring* Award
2013 Amazon Breakthrough Novel Awards—2nd place

Sybil Brakken, photo.

What readers say about James Brakken's writing:

"Wonderfully written .... Compelling" "A good piece of writing with suspense and action ..." **Jerry Apps, award-winning Wis. author**

"Weaving mystery into history, James Brakken's writing vivifies the tumultuous nature of 19th-century life in the legendary north woods." **Michael Perry, NYT bestselling Wisconsin author**

"Open with caution. You won't want to put this one down." **LaMoine MacLaughlin, President, Wisconsin Writers Association**

"A fascinating tale ... "Rip-roaring action ..." "So well-written." "Difficult to put down; a great read." **Publisher's Weekly Magazine**

"The writing style of this piece is its greatest strength." "The flow of the words is like an old fashioned song." **Amazon Books judge**

"It's the dialog and characters that drive The Treasure of Namakagon, a book that, if the audience for (adventure novels) was more like it was in the 1950s, would likely be sitting at or near the top of the best seller's lists. It appears as if author James A. Brakken is determined to make a go of this series, and ... he's made at least one fan of this reader." **Judge at 22nd Writer's Digest Book Awards**

"James Brakken has captured all of the current science, technology, and leadership necessary to preserve our lakes and streams." **Mary Platner, Founder and Past-president of WAL.**

"Brakken has provided a timely handbook for citizens ready to play their role in realizing the state's Public Trust Doctrine." **Eric Olson, Director, UW Extension Lakes**

"A twisting, thrilling mix of mystery, adventure and legendary treasure. Wisconsin history buffs will find this book a treasure in itself. An exciting adventure for all ages." **Waldo Asp, AARP Chairman**

"In scene after scene, the reader is surrounded by the beauty of pristine woods and lakes, rooting for the good guys to beat out the greedy." **A. Y. Stratton, author of Buried Heart**

"I liked it!" **Larry Meiller, Wisconsin Public Radio host.**

Made in the USA
Charleston, SC
13 June 2016